PERSONALITY Plus

Introducing You To You

By

Dr. Lynne O'Neill Hook, Ph.D.

Published by

R & E PUBLISHERS
P. O. Box 2008
Saratoga, California 95070

Typesetting by
Estella M. Krebs

Cover by
Kaye Graphics

Library of Congress Cataloging-in-Publication Data

Hook, Lynne O'Neill.
   Personality plus.

   Bibliography: p.
   1. Personality change. 2. Imagery (Psychology)
3. Success. I. Title.
BF698.2.H66 1986   158'.1   86-61606
ISBN 0-88247-760-9 (pbk.)

DEDICATED TO MY DAUGHTER

LYNNEMARIE

ACKNOWLEDGEMENT

This book is a synthesis of many ideas and philosophies learned in the study of psychology, and is intended for use by general readers. Extensive references have been omitted but there is a list of suggested readings.

Many people have contributed to my understanding of what promotes change in human personality and I would like to thank those from whom I have drawn ideas and inspiration. Greatly valued is the philosophical and psychological research data of my peers, both past and present.

It is my distinct pleasure to recognize and thank those individuals who have specifically contributed to this book.

Other writers will appreciate the fine support an author receives from the family, and it is my pleasure to thank my daughter, Lynnemarie Gibbons, and my son, Jay Hook, and especially my mother, Mrs. Mary O'Neill of England, for their loving support during the writing of this book.

Marilyn Baldwin, M.A.LMFCC, and Jan Peters, R.N. gave generously of their time and support and their friendship is appreciated. Support and friendship also came from Connie Conover, R.N., Donna Frasier, R.N., and Margaret Gurley.

Dr. John Wilson, doctoral advisor at Laurence University, Santa Barbara, gave the author invaluable assistance and support.

Colleagues who also contributed to my training are Erle Kirk, Ph.D., Deborah Ross, Ph.D., and William Yarbroff, Ph.D.

SUI GENERIS,
THE UNIQUENESS OF YOU

Within your inner self there is harmony where you can take time to savor the fullness of life and acknowledge your kinship with all humanity. Miracles within miracles are revealed as you journey through the timeless silence of your inner world and discover the mysteries of your mind.

Deep within yourself is a soothing stillness where you can see more clearly, hear more fully, and feel more deeply your own uniqueness. Images gently sculpt your highest dreams and shape them into realities.

You are always on the threshold of becoming something new, passing through seasons of sunshine and storm as you thrive and grow. Like seeds lovingly planted and cared for, whatever you create in the deeper recesses of your inner mind will blossom and grow and become reality. You have the capabilities and potential to succeed abundantly.

TABLE OF CONTENTS

INTRODUCTION

The idea of changing personality is an exhilarating one, as is the thought of sharing some exciting ideas with you for achieving the type of personality you desire. Through a dynamic cycle of rich imagery which leads to creative thinking, new emotions and fresh behaviors, you will develop your *PERSONALITY PLUS* in a way that is very pleasing to you.

PERSONALITY PLUS is a self-directed program, which will show you how to succeed using the new skills learned to overcome negative habit patterns. Please consider this as a challenge and give yourself every opportunity to use the skills described. This program will assist you to develop your personality in a way that will bring you more of life's rewards. This spiral of positive change begins with learning new skills to enhance your life. From learning a positive cycle of self-responsibility which results in increased self-esteem, you will be guided to an appreciation of your own self-worth. *PERSON-ALITY PLUS* uncovers that which is *sui generis*, unique, within you and enables you to blossom and share your fragrance with the world.

It is time now to introduce you to an important part of this program. The model selected for your *PERSONALITY PLUS* is that of a tall building. As a concept, *PERSONALITY PLUS* can be visualized as a new structure: utilizing many of your existing personality parts, expanding or deleting others, and adding many new features.

The higher you build the structure, the more levels you can incorporate into it and the more abundant your *PERSONALITY PLUS* will be. You will utilize your natural abilities and life experiences, and build on them to produce life satisfaction by incorporating ideas from this program into your life's activities. You will learn to expand upon the foundation, and grow from basement to penthouse thinking.

Give yourself every opportunity for success by mastering each new skill before proceeding with the next method. The broader the base you build, the greater the personal benefits. Shortcuts shortchange you. At the end of each chapter, before proceeding with the next one, go back and ask yourself if you have fully utilized your new learnings. *Patience:* you know that there is no shortcut through the forest of life. But there are ways to enjoy the glades, the trees, and the clearings by practicing each new skill until it becomes a part of your total personality. There is no direct ascent to the Penthouse Suite. You will be using a variety of creative skills to help you move from level to level, as appropriate, within the new personality structure you are building. At times, different levels are the most suitable for changing situations. Cultivating the ability to master the levels puts them at your disposal when needed. Take a moment now to examine, on page 3, the *PERSONALITY PLUS* you will be building.

PERSONALITY PLUS BUILDING

Level 10	Penthouse Suite	Your highest level of competency.
Level 9	Upper Level II	Refining interpersonal behaviors and recognition of the barometer of your comfort, your popularity and ability to share.
Level 8	Upper Level I	Freshening interpersonal behaviors by assertively communicating to empower yourself.
Level 7	Intermediate Level II	Creatively using your thoughts as powerful tools.
Level 6	Intermediate Level I	Affirming humor, happiness, power, love, mastery, philosophy and pleasure, and enhancing self-esteem.
Level 5	Primary Level II	Overcoming anxiety, grief and pain, and learning courage and compassion.
Level 4	Primary Level I	Introducing complexity and growth with rich imagery.
Level 3	Ground Level	Discovering your own daimonic potential.
Level 2	Basement Level	Developing positive emotions and enhancing your self image.
Level 1	Foundation of your personality	Building a new structure on the existing foundation of your personality.

The *PERSONALITY PLUS* program will work if you use it individually by being self-reliant; for it is the personal work which, in the long run, makes the change. The program will also work if you choose to do it with a close friend, where you can share ideas and chart each other's progress. If you are in a support group, this information is most helpful as a group project. If you are working with a professional, these ideas can be incorporated into the overall therapy plan. You will be building a positive spiral of thoughts, emotions and behaviors to enrich your life. You can learn to control those aspects of your personality which damage your relationships, and take the best of yourself and improve that. You will be learning to drop off negative personality traits by changing habits, and learning skills to develop positive personality traits to increase self-satisfaction.

Rich imagery, to transform negative into positive emotions, with increased creative thinking and enhanced behaviors, runs like a golden thread throughout the tapestry of your personality, and will work to create a change in all areas of your life. With new skills you will facilitate your growth in two directions. On the one hand, you can allow your personality to unfold at its own speed in the deep, inner recesses of your mind, like a flower opening up to the morning sun, and you will benefit from that. This growth, which unfolds effortlessly from within, is enhanced by the methods which you will learn, and the work you do will pay dividends. On the other hand, the active skills will include examining your whole life and actively choosing to change your thoughts, emotions and behaviors until new habits are formed. A flexible approach in both directions maximizes your growth. Be kind to yourself as you nurture your own growth. It is possible to go through life with blinders on to your own potential. This program is designed to enlarge your vision, expand your self-awareness, and enrich your personality with new ideas.

You will build your *PERSONALITY PLUS* by creating it floor by floor. You will make some of these changes immediately with rich imagery and Journal work, and noticing the various levels existing in your personality at present. You will become aware when you are operating on a lower level than is necessary for you to get what you want out of life. The prospect of your inner growth is exciting, and can lead to more satisfying relationships with significant others as well as yourself.

Building on the foundation of your personality, you have the choice of working with the information stored in your brain or choosing to enhance your brainpower by adding new ideas and experiences. View the *PERSONALITY PLUS* concepts and skills as being given brand new tools. If you leave the tools unused, they will not benefit you at all. Read this book through to the end if you wish, but it is essential that you come back to the beginning and start incorporating the exercises and ideas into your personality in a meaningful way. Look on this as an exciting challenge, an opportunity to work on yourself to create a personality that will please you immensely and enhance your life. Growth is a lifetime process.

LEVEL 1: FOUNDATION LEVEL

Your Existing Personality

The foundation of your personality can be as solid as you choose to make it. Your personality was formed originally by others' view of you, and your own self-view. Your personality can be changed by improving your own self-view, which will improve the way others' perceive and treat you. Your foundation can be strengthened by mastering the following skills:

1. Journal writing   — using advanced imagery methods
2. Positive emotions — from creative thinking
3. Rich imagery   — to increase creativity
4. Creative thinking — left and right brain functioning
5. Fresh behaviors   — to elicit new behaviors from others

Journal writing will start your initial personality changes, and will later document for you when the changes occurred. Positive emotions occur as you change your thinking, and rich imagery will develop by increasing your sensory awareness. Higher levels of brain integration evolve anew from creative thinking. The fresh behaviors which result will improve your relationships with significant others, and will result in your ability to operate at your highest level of competency. Your conscious mind contains approximately 10 percent of your abilities while the other 90 percent exists in your subconscious mind. You can learn to access more of your brainpower, and use this incredible knowledge to achieve what you want out of life.

With the *PERSONALITY PLUS* program, you can feed information from your conscious mind to your inner, deeper subconscious mind. This happens outside your awareness automatically from all your experiences. However, why let it happen haphazardly, and perhaps in a negative direction, when with a little effort you can program your subconscious deeper mind in a positive direction by using *PERSONALITY PLUS* skills? Each time you alter the level on which you operate in the world, you do more than change levels. You are altering the fundamental foundation on which your personality is built.

For Journal writing, obtain a loose-leafed binder of lined paper to use as your Journal. Date your entries and later you will be able to see your progress. Right now take responsibility for making a solid personality foundation using this Journal. Written Journal work involves incorporating all of the skills you are learning as you progress through the program. Many senses are involved in writing and this work will solidify your intention to make the changes you desire. It will allow you to keep track of your progress, and will motivate you towards further change. Making a contract privately with yourself, or with someone who is close to you, will sustain your motivation to reach your chosen goals. Set your goals by:

1. Choosing a realistic date some time from now when you expect this personality change to be noticeable to yourself and others.
2. Utilizing all your skills of reading, writing, drawing or painting, and adding them to the skills in this book to achieve your goals.
3. Moving from self-to-other centeredness. To the extent you

are able to balance your needs, and the needs of others, you exhibit maturity. Early thought processes were self-centered, but they can be changed as maturity develops through self-mastery.

4. Choosing people to spend time with who will help you reach your goals.

5. Giving yourself token rewards, and planning one major reward as you reach pinnacles of success.

Journal writing is enhanced with rich imagery, which can commence with a feeling that you are descending into a safe, comfortable and warm place inside yourself. You can put a relaxing countdown on tape, or just use the numbers to count backwards to relax yourself. To assist you to reach a deep level of relaxation *before any imagery*: close your eyes, relax your mouth and jaw, and visualize a blue lake before your eyes — one that fills the whole screen. Drop your shoulders and support yourself with your breathing. Breathing naturally, give yourself permission to enjoy this experience of deep relaxation. Allow all the cares of the day to drift effortlessly away. As you relax, feel the warmth of your body. Drifting deeper and deeper into the center core of yourself, start to count silently to yourself (or play your tape of it):

10   as you float gently down. . .

9   you are aware of a great sense of peace. . .

8   your body and mind begin to relax. . .

7   as you experience joy within yourself. . .

6   as you gently drift and drift. . .

5   and you become aware of sounds that please you. . .

4   and you feel more at ease than you have ever felt before. . .

3   for you feel so comfortable, peaceful and serene. . .

2   as you relax totally and completely. . .

1   you experience happiness and deep relaxation. . .

Rich imagery will start you on your journey into your inner consciousness. Every long journey begins with the first small step, as does every change you make in yourself. Most of the building blocks to personality change come from the inner you, and rich imagery is a very effective method for making these changes. New visualizations will aid you in accomplishing your goals. In examining your personality, there may be areas you will want to keep and others you would like to change completely, or there might be a distinctly different type of personality which appeals to you which you can aim for.

Rich imagery includes using all your senses: sight, sound, smell, taste, touch, and your emotions. Using the following method, write in full detail in your Journal, the way you desire your personality to be:

1. *Sight:* How will you look? Write in detail how your new personality will look to yourself and others. See yourself behaving and thinking in ways that will incorporate the skills as you learn them. Write down each specific skill you will be practicing, and see yourself doing that skill successfully in imagery.

2. *Sound:* How will you sound? Write out sentences you plan to practice, such as "I'd be smiling and talking confidently." Describe hearing someone complimenting you. In imagery, hear the sounds of your successfully handling situations.

3. *Smell:* What will the aromas be? Write about the pleasant smells you would like present, such as your favorite flowers or perfume. Or choose a pleasant smell where someone has baked a treat for you as a result of your new behaviors. Add any other aroma you love.

4. *Taste:* What will you taste? Can you taste the baked food? Perhaps you will write about the taste of success.

5. *Touch:* What touches will change? Can you imagine being

gently touched or tenderly touching someone else?

6. *Emotions:* What emotions do you want present? With your new personality, describe the different emotions you will experience, such as joy, peace or satisfaction.

In the deeper recesses of your subconscious mind, you have untold resources. In a private place where you will be left alone, close your eyes and go within and listen to the answers which you need to several important questions. Relax yourself deeply, and begin to notice your breathing and ask yourself, being very specific:

1.	What is it I want?	Describe it fully.
2.	Why do I want this?	Giving meaning to your goals.
3.	Where would be best?	Narrowing the focus.
4.	With whom do I choose to be?	Alone or with others.
5.	When is the best time for it?	Timing is crucial sometimes.
6.	How can I get it?	Allow strategies to develop.

The more specific you can be, the more easily you will know when you are successful. If you choose happiness, for example, be specific and state what *you* mean by happiness. The more concretely you can formulate your ideas, the more easily you will be able to magnetize ideas about how to accomplish your goals.

When you have written the answers to the above questions in your Journal, let a little time pass. In this time, allow your ideas to percolate in your mind. Mull over the alternatives to what you have chosen to make sure you have not overlooked any important aspects of your future. When you get additional inspirations for yourself, add them to the list. Revise your ideas as often as is necessary; nothing is set in concrete until you decide it is. Once you have formulated clearly what it is you want for yourself, then concentrate on how you can get it. The more alternatives you can generate

11

and put into practice immediately, the more likely you are to achieve your goals.

Choosing your personality changes can be accomplished by:

1. Remembering a peak experience, a few minutes of time, when your accomplishments made you feel exhilarated. Write out this experience as though it were happening right now. After you have written every detail of that experience, sum it up in a few sentences that show how powerful you felt, and underline it in your Journal.

2. Visualizing something you want a great deal, write a full, complete scenario as if the event was actually happening right now.

3. Obtaining a picture of someone you would choose to be like; not necessarily look like, but to resemble in personality. From this picture, write out all the things you admire about this individual, and the ways you would like to create them in yourself.

Until you have a clear picture of the changes you desire, you have nothing to measure them against later. Perhaps you might choose to be a composite of several people, taking the best features of all of them. The purpose of writing out your plan is to convey to the deepest reaches of your brain the exact changes you are aiming for. Write out all the things you want to achieve in your personality change, working on it until you are satisfied with them.

Your own creativity can suggest enriched imagery that will help you to accomplish your goals. Simply examine one aspect of your personality at a time. After you have the goal, describe how you will know that you have achieved the goal. The stronger you can visualize yourself in imagery with the desired personality, the more successful you will be. In your Journal, please write:

1. Your goal, and the small steps you plan to make.

2. A full description of your new personality using enriched imagery.
3. What rewards you plan to give yourself for the new behavior.

As you become more skilled progressing through the book, add to the items in your Journal. The new personality you can richly imagine for yourself is your *PERSONALITY PLUS* which, when added to the other new skills you will learn in this program, will assist you to make the desired changes.

When you have written out a complete description of your desired new personality in your Journal as described above, please find a quiet place where you can be alone. Close your eyes and relax deeply by concentrating on your breathing, and remembering any other time when you have been totally relaxed. Then, mentally form an image of yourself the way you would like to be as though it existed already. Make it as strong and rich an imagery as possible. For the next few weeks I want you to spend quiet time visualizing this rich image of yourself. Set a time, such as after shutting off the alarm in the morning, or before going to sleep at night when you shut off the light, and fully visualize and experience your new personality. Remember to do it as though it existed now. Experience yourself with all the vivid attributes you desire. An image formed in your mind attracts other similar images. Please be sure to revise your personality as new ideas occur to you. Don't settle for part of a new personality when you can have it all – your own *PERSONALITY PLUS*.

Changing your personality is similar to stepping into the space surrounding your inner self. What occurs is that you make a paradigm shift. Instead of seeing your world with limited boundaries, you expand your world view and shift to a different parameter. The paradigm shift in your personality would be similar to the changes of first, seeing the earth as flat – then seeing it as round – and later being able to view the world from outer space. You are radically altering and extending your self-view and your personality. However, you are expanding your *inner* self-knowledge to achieve it.

The way out of many of life's difficulties is learning the ability to step outside the situation you are in and view that situation from a more global perspective. Some relationships are like two trees planted too close together that know little of the forest and even less of the world beyond that. The ability to comment on the fact that perhaps the two trees involved just might obstruct each others' views and growth involves a major shift in looking at your relationships. Learning to replant yourself in a relationship and taking responsibility for your own growth while maintaining interdependency in relationships strengthens foundations.

Maturity then begins with going deeper inside oneself, and nurturing your own individuality in order to obtain gifts to give to others. If your own well is dry, there is no water for others; going deep inside yourself allows the wellspring to fill you up to overflowing and you can share the abundance. Each time you allow yourself quiet time to meditate or do relaxation exercises, you allow the process of self-healing to occur. Each time you cue yourself to perform your rich imagery exercises and write in your Journal, you are separating yourself from those around you and carving for yourself the type of personality and relationships you desire. Stay on track every day taking small steps toward your goals for achieving what you want out of life.

Growth involves living with self-discovery and change. Any time you are faced with a transition from one stage of your life to another, it is as though you were rooted on the spot looking both backwards at your past security and forwards to the unknown. This creates anxiety as you look at real or imagined threats to your security. The potential for growth, which is emerging, destroys your present security and you must control your anxiety to keep alive the new opportunities which are opening up for you.

The aim of *PERSONALITY PLUS* is psychological maturity, and all authorities agree this contains three overlapping areas. You must have: (1) *conscious knowledge of yourself,* (2) *your world,* and (3) *suitable work in accordance with this knowledge.* Conscious knowledge of yourself includes awareness of your subconscious abilities. Conscious knowledge of your world means seeing realistically the world in which you live. Suitable work based on knowledge of yourself and your world involves discovering what your life work is.

You cannot achieve this by reading this or any other book. From the step-by-step processes in this book, however, valuable methods are described which can lead to personality changes to improve your interpersonal relationships and personal happiness. Your efforts contribute to your life happiness by showing you ways that you can enhance and appreciate your unique self-worth. *PERSONALITY PLUS* will teach you ways to enjoy your human birthright and give you access to your own potential in the process of self-discovery.

Into your personality structure build flexibility in every direction. Avoid rigidity and old ways of thinking. Learn to expand on the ideas presented here as appropriate for your own uniqueness. Discovering areas about yourself not included here gives you a measure of self-awareness from which to grow. Accept those levels of your personality which enhance your life now, making sure to maintain flexibility as you add new dimensions in the future.

Take a moment here to evaluate what you have learned about yourself so far by answering these points in your Journal:

- What have I learned about myself?
- In what ways am I different than I thought?
- Who are the people I value in my life?
- What do I value about myself?
- Where am I going with my life?
- Who can assist me to get there, and who can I assist?
- How can I overcome discovered areas of weakness?
- Where are my strengths and capabilities?

- Am I spending enough time on the exercises?
- Will I give myself every opportunity to perform the exercises?
- Am I reaching high enough in my aspirations?
- When will my subconscious reveal to my conscious mind those things which are beneficial to me?
- How does my *PERSONALITY PLUS* grow?

From the work you have done to date, congratulate yourself, and eagerly turn to the following levels to learn new skills to achieve your highest potential. At the end of *each* chapter, carefully review the material to make sure that you have covered all the steps for self-actualization. This is your opportunity to increase your interpersonal effectiveness to achieve *PERSONALITY PLUS*.

LEVEL 2: BASEMENT LEVEL

Positive Emotions

Now that you are working on your daily Journal writing, dating your entries to chart your progress, and using rich creative imagery to change your self-picture in the deeper recesses of your creative subconscious mind, you may be noticing pleasing changes in your personality and in your significant relationships. As you change your life perspectives in small, steady increments, you become aware of your potential to achieve increasingly higher levels of performance.

You are now ready to explore the basement level, and to choose positive, rather than negative thinking. Basement thinking involves the chaos of positive and negative thinking swirling through your head and where, without effort, negative thinking will prevail. Worse yet, if it is allowed to continue, negative thinking produces negative emotions which are painful and depressing. You can choose to consciously feed your mind a stream of positive emotions from rational thinking, which will attract other positive ideas, or allow your negative thinking to prevail. Feelings come from the way you think. For example, try to get angry with someone without thinking about it.

By examining your thought processes, you have the power to

control, use and harmonize all your senses. You can direct your thoughts, control your thinking, and master your life in a powerful way. Opening up your mind to flexible alternatives for dealing with conflicts permits you to make better choices. Remember please that how you think determines how you feel — without question and at all times. Positive and negative emotions cannot occupy your mind at the same time, and you have a choice, every minute of the day, in which direction your emotions will go. Both emotions begin minor and will become all pervasive and the spiral might look like this:

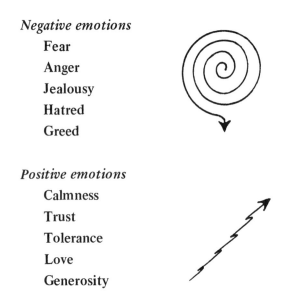

Negative emotions
    Fear
    Anger
    Jealousy
    Hatred
    Greed

Positive emotions
    Calmness
    Trust
    Tolerance
    Love
    Generosity

Whichever direction you allow your thoughts to follow, in time, the mind tape will run in that direction without any further conscious thought from you. You owe it to yourself to learn to feed your inner mind a series of positive thoughts so that you can enjoy positive emotions every day.

Your task in this program is to reach a higher level of operating, moving up to the penthouse suite by occupying levels in your personality which are the most advantageous to you. Albert Ellis, a psychologist, very expertly describes how negative thinking produces negative emotions. Positive thinking will produce positive and healthy emotions. You are being asked to make a major shift: moving from old belief systems to new belief systems. You do not get depressed or angry from nowhere; these emotions are a direct result of what you are thinking.

Ellis views humans as both rational and irrational. Repeated ideas, either negative or positive, will produce that type of emotion. He teaches that life events may be uncontrollable, but you have a choice in the way you react to them. Rational thinking begins with separating a person's actions from the person himself. What a person does is different from what a person is. You build your self-image with the way you think about yourself, and you build relationships by how you think about others. It may be only one event which lowers esteem of yourself or others, but it is the repetitious thoughts about the event which fills you with negative emotion. The mind, like the computer, will operate on Garbage In/Garbage Out. Your self-talk controls your thoughts which, in turn, control your behavior. Changing the ways you think will change the way you act. Your judgment of events is what bothers your mind. When you are distressed, it is pointless to blame other people; it is more productive to examine your judgment of events. Escaping from basement thinking involves using your mind to promote Excellence In/Excellence Out in your thinking processes.

Positive emotions can replace negative emotions by using imagery in the following way, either taping or reading the exercise: Close your eyes, concentrating on your breathing and extending the exhalation by counting to yourself as you breathe out. Allow your breathing to support you as you drift into a state of deep relaxation.

Brand R

Experience a feeling of calmness, stillness and peace, with a deep sense of serenity. You feel lighter, and an upswing in energy as you experience enthusiasm, vitality, good health, acceptance, love, success and happiness. Feel the energy field expand as you experience the parts of you which are strong, and becoming even stronger. You are feeling fine, and your heart is full of contentment, love and joy. Floating even higher, you experience the deeper knowing of your own potential for harmony with life. Allow these feelings to permeate your entire being, and bring these emotions back into the room with you.

Brand X

Experience a feeling of self-rejection, guilt, tiredness and disappointment. Become aware of anger, worry and fear, and notice the depressed sensations which spread gloom throughout your body. Notice a feeling of rejection and disappointment. Everything is black and dreary and your body is filled with a feeling of hopelessness. Become aware of a feeling of constriction as you withdraw into a world of misery and unhappiness. You are surrounded by hurt and pain, and everywhere is filled with darkness and gloom. Your spirit is heavily laden and sad.

Do not allow these feelings to permeate your entire being, instead repeat Exercise R, and strongly notice the difference.

Brand X is an example of what we can do to ourselves by allowing negative tapes to run in a negative direction for many hours. If the tape in your head resembles Brand X, your thought processes are producing negative emotions. Simply changing the tape to Brand R defeats Brand X. *Brand X should only ever be done once as an experiment, and then abandoned forever.* It is important to feed your mind good, healthy thoughts of being full of energy, enthusiasm and vitality. Allow yourself to stay in good health, feeling fine, with a heart full of happiness, love and joy.

Depression can be viewed as a time of recouping but, instead of permitting the clouds of depression to hang around, actively change your thought processes to produce positive emotions. Should you at first experience difficulty going from negative to positive thoughts, learn the power of slipping into neutral thinking by changing the subject of your thinking. If the only way you can stop the negative tape is to choose not to have an opinion on a subject that is upsetting you, then do that by going into neutral temporarily. With practice, your thought processes will learn to change into positive thinking.

A very successful exercise for dealing with, say, anger is to imagine that it is escaping through your head as steam. Doing it in the exact situation where the anger is occurring is very helpful. Noticing another person's anger, and visualizing them with steam coming from their heads, will help you to reject the anger as being directed to you. As another device, you can choose to place a shield between their anger and you.

The left and right brain handle different things, and good health physically and mentally means paying close attention to left-brain thinking processes. Learn to listen to the dialogue between self-and-self, or self-and-others, and change it to beneficial thinking. You may sometimes harm others as a result of what you think, but you *always* harm yourself by negative thoughts. Remember, the left brain, which thinks in words, handles the intellectual functions, and the right brain, which thinks in images, handles the emotional functions. Both sides of the brain can be cemented together by making your left brain *chief executive* and putting it in charge of your emotions. You can learn to do this by monitoring your self talk. Instead of letting your thoughts run amok, pay close attention to what you are thinking, and immediately change thoughts which are damaging to you.

Where the thought patterns are not changed, and the emotions run wild —whether overtly or covertly — whether they are noticeable to other people or not, great bodily damage can occur. If thoughts are not handled at the beginning, they produce emotions, which in turn produce damage to your body. Your language is organ language, and it pays to take great care what you say to yourself. For example, if you say "I am heartbroken" repeatedly to yourself, you might as well prepare for heart surgery. People talk about "Not being able to stomach someone or something," or "Wish that people would get off my back." All of these self-statements can result in damage to that part of the body. People with skin complaints itch to get away or out of relationships, unaware that what they are saying to themselves is causing the skin damage.

Negative emotions can be very effectively dealt with using the following imagery:

Ruler of the Universe

Imagine that you are ruler of the universe, and as such you have complete and absolute control over everyone in the world. Now think of an event or a person who caused you a great deal of painful emotion, and feel all the anger you feel towards that event or person. Remember clearly everything he/she did to you. Now, imagine that this person is being brought before you by two of your subjects, and you can do anything at all that you wish to that person, without fear of punishment.

Nothing that you do can hurt that person in real life, but in imagery you can deal with the issue once and for all. Make sure that you are completely satisfied with the outcome, and have a feeling of closure about the event. Someone once asked me whether I believed a deed committed in imagery was the same as a deed committed in real life, and I remember replying, "If I told you I have given $10,000 or a blank check to your church *in imagery*, would you give me the credit for doing it?" I believe that if we don't get the credit for the good we might do in imagery, we cannot get the discredit for the negative either.

In using imagery to deal with negative emotions, you are relieving yourself of negative thoughts and carrying tension around in your body over unresolved conflict. It is a way of recognizing your negative potential and acknowledging it without acting on it in reality. In the past, you may have heard of imagining a sports event in order to improve your game; i.e., doing something in imagination to improve real events. This method is the other side of the coin, doing something in imagination so that it will not be necessary to take action in reality. Both methods are effective in improving how you perform in the real world.

How change occurs is the subject of much debate. People who seek to make changes and don't are facing the same law of energy that any object of enertia versus motion does. An object at rest must have sufficient energy applied to it to overcome inertia. Once inertia is overcome, movement and progress begin. But where, you might ask, does energy come from to overcome inertia in people? First, let us examine how this happens spontaneously. A strong negative emotion, such as hate or anger, will energize a person to negative action. A strong, positive emotion, such as passionate love or enthusiasm, will energize a person to positive action. This can be observed in spontaneous emotions, but we have yet to apply this knowledge to overcome inertia intentionally.

Learn to appreciate the power of your ideas. An idea, combined with energy supplied by emotion, an energized idea, will overcome inertia in the following way. Depending on whether you allow strong negative or positive thinking to produce your emotional mind-set, you will be energized in one direction or another. By improving and expanding your thinking, and using the skills outlined in this book, you can energize your creative abilities, and you can succeed in making changes and overcoming inertia. An energized idea magnetizes other similar ideas to it, and from this additional energy, change will also occur.

For example, if you actively produce positive emotions by monitoring your thinking, and you practice creative imagery to change your behaviors, you will be producing a mind-set and behavior change which will produce other similar healthy habits. While you continue with your Journal writing, and imagery to reach your future goals, let the melody from these skills lead you into energized action to build a *PERSONALITY PLUS*.

In this program, you will learn how important it is to separate yourself from those people you are related to. It is a necessary part of maturing. The more effectively you separate emotionally and intellectually, the more you can reintegrate with family, friends and partners on a more mature level. Each time you change your views to a higher level of thinking and behaving, your brain retains the memory and will use this information in future situations. What may begin as awkward first steps towards change will, with time, become smooth and comfortable ways of thinking and behaving. The more self-awareness you achieve, and the greater number of skills you practice, the firmer the foundation you will have on which to build your *PERSONALITY PLUS*.

Change is rarely made in a straight line upwards, it more closely resembles an irregular pattern of ups and downs, in an upward direction. Change can be made by building readiness and learning to support and assist yourself. You can assist inner strengthening, but time is needed for the process to occur. There are three levels of change: Minor ones such as clothes, or the same job elsewhere. Major ones in thoughts, attitudes or perceptions. Then there is change at the Transformative level, becoming a different person than you were before. Communicating with yourself about *YOU* accelerates the process of change.

Unconsciously you might have experienced a sense of needing to change your personality, and awareness comes as you recognize the need for change – which might have begun with purchasing this book. From chaotic uncertainty, there arises a dynamic tension which must occur in order to grow. You must then formulate a vision of what you want to change and how, and implement the change in your daily living. Integration occurs when you combine the skills learned in this program and make them your own to protect yourself. Whatever you imagine can work to reduce the anger. For working on other negative emotions, such as hate, greed, jealousy or anxiety, allow yourself first to reach a deep level of relaxation. Then imagine that you are standing under a shower. In examining yourself undressed, imagine that you can see the negative emotion exuding from your body, perhaps as a thick crusty fluid, and as you see it, turn on the shower and imagine that it is washing away all of the emotions which are harmful to you and to other people. Check to be sure it is all gone. Stand under the shower until you can see your whole body, fresh and clean, while you experience what it feels like to have all of the negative emotions drained out of your body down the drain, far away from you.

There are many ways you can imagine this cleansing of negative emotions. You can see a strong jet of fluid flushing the thick crusty fluid away, you can see a warm sun melting the negative emotions from your skin and draining away, or you can imagine a heat lamp dissolving all the tension and negativity and drying up all the painful emotions. Any method that your creative mind suggests is the right method for you. Any method that allows you to feel that the negative emotions have been eradicated from your body is ideal, and may be practiced as often as necessary.

Negative emotions are held in the muscle tissue, this tension creates pain, and this pain causes more muscle tension. To break this negative cycle, any one of the above methods for dealing with unwanted emotions will give you relief, and more importantly, will teach you how to control your emotions. Self-control increases self-esteem, and self-esteem increases positive thinking which improves your ability to control your emotions. Working on this positive cycle removes the harmful stress which negative thinking pours into your bloodstream. You are worth the effort, and the rewards are gratifying.

Mastery and self-control of thinking and emotions commences with learning which parts of your personality are allies and which are adversaries. Make sure you learn to conquer the adversarial parts, while at the same time joining hands with the allies within yourself. Make a list in your Journal of those allies you plan to increase, and those adversaries you plan to conquer. For example, your adversaries might include: low self-esteem, anxiety, anger, fear, stress, guilt, or depression. As well as passivity, unrealistic expectations, perfectionism, and self-defeating attitudes. Your allies might be perserverance, a sense of humor, motivation, high self-esteem, positive emotions and determination to master self-control. In your imagination, seek to find your Imagery Ally, and however you describe her/him, recognize that this is your own power.

You can model your Imagery Ally after a personality that you admire, and mold it to your unique individuality. Pick someone who seems to have mastered problems that you would like to find the solution to, and model yourself after them. Practice the skills the other person has until they become your own. Allow yourself to flow from basement to penthouse thinking and choose what you want of life. Whatever you practice in your mind, your body learns to do. Thoughts create reality, and thinking of eliminating adversarial agents and increasing your allies will make them a reality.

LEVEL 3: GROUND LEVEL
Your Daimonic Potential

Daimonic

This level is concerned with introducing a model of personality which has been described using many different terms. Rollo May chose the concept of the daimonic, and defined happiness as the ability to live in harmony with it. He described the daimonic as both creative and destructive, and stressed the importance of integrating the daimonic into the total personality. It is unacceptable to our pride and narcissism, and our self-view that we are "civilized," to admit our savage impulses exist. However, until we acknowledge both good and evil impulses within and stop repressing the acknowledgement of the evil, there is the possibility that it will erupt and be destructive.

For every good thing acknowledged in the personality, there exists its opposite. The more you can recognize your full personality, the healthier your relationship with yourself and others will be. Being willing to acknowledge the full personality is all that is required; it is unnecessary to act out the destructive elements. In Figure 1, mark those items which you feel represent your daimonic potential. Having awareness of the destructive elements and ackknowledging our similarities to each other is all that is required for healthy self-awareness. Maturity involves tolerating the anxiety of your capacity for both good and evil, and not running away from it. As human beings, we are capable of the full spectrum of emotions from the most self-sacrificing love to the deepest hatred and cruelty. Instead of using energy to deny your negative impulses, it is healthful to get in touch with the opposites and contradictions in your personality. This can be done by dealing with negative impulses using imagery. The more rapidly you deal with the negative impulse, the quicker you can adjust to the stressful emotion. Your task is to promote the positive in your personality, and accept self-responsibility to reach your highest potential.

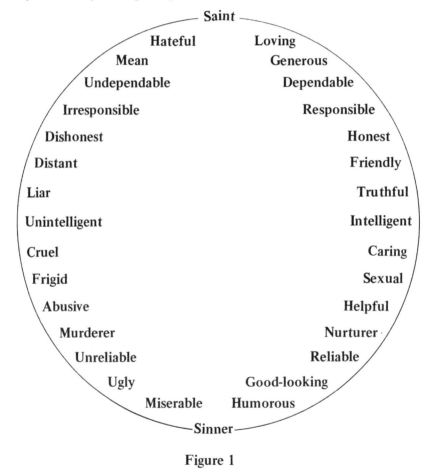

Figure 1

How many of the above parts of your personality are you willing to accept as being part of your potential? In your Journal, write and date how many you agree with about yourself and notice if your ability to recognize other personality parts increases with time. There is no need to act upon the negatives within, merely be aware of them as possibilities. Instead of feeling alienated from others who have acted on their negative impulses, you will understand them and feel closer to other human beings.

One of my patients was a mother with two small children. Her view of herself was that she was loving and kind, and that she had no negative traits. As long as she tried to keep that picture of herself intact, she experienced great difficulty with her anger towards her boys when they misbehaved. Once she learned to accept her anger as a valid part of the range of emotions she must deal with, this act put her in touch with her negative and positive feelings.

Another way to deal with negative emotions, such as anger, is to sit somewhere privately and say these words to yourself silently, while feeling in your body the emotions they arouse:

> *I have the potential to be a very angry person. However, I choose to let all my anger drain away. I choose to stop being angry with myself, my parents, with others, and with all the people from the past and the present.*
>
> *When I experience anger in the future, I will choose merely to acknowledge it, and to deal with it immediately by choosing to let it go. Negative emotions, such as anger, are stressful to my body and I choose to deal with them in this way to enhance my life. I choose positive emotions, such as humor and laughter.*

Experiencing the words in your body, not merely thinking them, helps the process of self-healing. A great deal of energy is used when negative emotions are hidden from awareness. Coming to terms with your depths will enable you to experience your heights. To make your life vital and full of meaning, you need to be connected to the core feelings within yourself. Learning to live comfortably with your full human personality prevents the negative potential from turning sour and working against you. You are learning, in this way, self-control and mastery when you are actively controlling the destructive urges, and expressing the creative within.

Choosing to love only would be preferred by most people. Picking up love, however, is like picking up a coin — there is hate on the reverse side. Only the people you love have the power to strongly frustrate you, and that frustration is what causes anger and hatred. The opposite of love is not hate, it is indifference. Love is intertwined with hate. While emotions are raging, you experience both sides of the coin. For each personal interaction of importance you mentally flip the coin, and how you think about the situation will determine your emotions. The task in good relationships is to make sure that the love side of the coin comes up the most often.

Holding on to the mythical idea of "pure love" creates a great deal of heartache. When you believe that a good relationship only involves positive emotions, what you believe runs counter to what is true of human beings. A great deal of unnecessary pain is created by expecting to give and receive pure love. Having the ability to acknowledge the power of opposing emotions enables you to choose to adjust your thinking to produce loving emotions. This is not only for the benefit of the other person but also it is for your own benefit. As long as you are struggling with conflicting emotions, you are stressing your body and mind and it is in your best interest to resolve the issue.

Going within yourself and telling the truth about the situation can enable you to resolve the problem. For example, admitting that someone made you very, very angry by their behavior, but that you love them as a person, will help you to see how it is possible to have two opposing opinions about a person at the same time. You can then choose which emotion you wish to hold on to. In flipping the coin, see how many times you can make the love side come up if you want to maintain a loving relationship.

Helium Balloon

A powerful method for producing positive emotions is to visualize a helium balloon and practice any of the following:

1. *Imagine that you are connected to the helium balloon by tubes. Turn all the negative emotions to liquid and imagine the liquid draining out from your body into the helium balloon.*

2. *Visualize that the helium balloon has a strong laser light which can draw negativity from your body, and experience all the emotions draining away.*

3. *With any pain, imagine that you can turn on faucets in your fingers and toes, and allow the pain to drain along the tubes into the balloon.*

4. *View all of your past experiences as being on tapes in your head in the form of videotapes and audiotapes, and when you find yourself running these tapes through your head, instead imagine that they can be taped into the balloon. Clearing out old sounds and pictures gives you the opportunity to enjoy the present and future.*

When you have drained the experiences in visualization, it is then very important that you complete the exercise by imagining the helium balloon rising in the sky, higher and higher, until it reaches outer space. See, hear and feel the disintegration of the helium balloon and all your negative emotions and thinking. Experience it in your body, knowing that if the negativity has not completely drained away, you have the capacity to keep on filling helium balloons until it does.

Court Case

To continue the task of changing your personality from basement level to higher level thinking, please ask yourself whether you are involved in a Court Case by taking one of the following positions:

Defendant: Does the tape running through your head constantly prove to you that you are right? If you are explaining to yourself or others at length, you are playing Defendant.

Sometimes the more you explain the less convincing you are, and recognizing this can be liberating. Instead, make one simple explanation and then drop the issue. Listen, instead of debating the issue.

Prosecutor: Do you blame yourself and others harshly, and often unnecessarily? Do you have an endless tape running through your head that blames yourself or the whole world for what is going on? If you made a mistake, or others did, and you are constantly putting yourself and others down, then you are playing Prosecutor.

Recognize this blaming process, and become aware how much it interferes with interpersonal relations. Stop expecting perfection from yourself and others. You are not an angel or devil, just a human being doing the best you can.

Jury: Do you bring in outsiders to support your point of view in arguments? Do you say, "Everyone else. . . . ," or "All the people in work or school . . . . ." When you quote others to support your position, you are playing Jury.

The less you rely on the mythical "everybody" to convince someone else, the further you will be from calling in a Jury. Learn to get in touch with your own inner convictions.

Judge: *When you hear someone else's point of view, do you judge them and their behavior as though you were a Supreme Court Judge? If you condemn yourself or others for their actions, you are probably playing hanging Judge.*

Become aware when you are being "omnipotent" and judging others. Stop labeling others' behavior and recognize that in their situation you may have behaved the same way.

Silence is a powerfully convincing tool. Begin to silence your own defendant, prosecuting, jury and judging tendencies. If right now you are endlessly explaining to yourself how right you are and saying "I never do that," this is an excellent example of defending yourself internally.

Stop Sign Magic

Putting up a stop sign, mentally, in your head is a first step in resting the case against yourself and others. Quickly say silently *STOP*, and begin your ascent to a higher level of thinking. Record your successes in your Journal each time you successfully conquer playing Court Case. Make sure to reward yourself for your successes, and forgive yourself for any lapses. Pick a reward that you will give yourself on the day you are successful, and thoroughly enjoy the treat.

LEVEL 4:   PRIMARY LEVEL I
Rich Imagery

As the structure grows taller, you begin to use more sophisticated tools in order to sustain the increasing complexity of your imagination. You have *within yourself* the power to transform the quality of your life. You may have already discovered that Rich Imagery is a very effective tool for reaching higher levels in your personality structure. It can also be used to improve your physiological and psychological health. From the imagery work begun and recorded in your Journal, you may becoming aware of the ways it can alert you to achieve your own excellence. In addition, for use in health, imagery is proving effective when used in addition to medication to strengthen the immune system against disease. It is widely used in stress control and habit reduction.

Roger Sperry, in 1981, was awarded the Nobel Prize for Medicine for his research on the difference between right and left brain functions. In about 95% of people, the left brain is the logical hemisphere, and is dominant for verbal, analytical and linear tasks and controls the opposite side of the body for movements. Imagery emerges from the nonverbal right brain, which is the base of your creativity, intuition and it sees things holistically. The right brain, because it has no language, uses imagery and symbols instead. Wiggle your left thumb right now; it was the right brain which gave those instructions. You use your right brain constantly, mostly outside of your awareness. Rich imagery is a way to increase right-brain activities, and improve brain synchronization.

Right brain imagery can be improved by taping the following sentences to enhance your skills:

See a magnificent forest scene, with majestic pine trees. . .

Visualize a long, lazy river, and smell the clear water flowing by. . .

Now see white rapids as they roar across the river rocks. . .

Imagine a glorious lake view. Feel the sunshine on your arms. . .

Look at the beautiful, blue sky, and notice the white fluffy clouds. . .

Imagine your favorite campground. Smell and taste your favorite cookout. . .

Imagine a tropical beach with palm trees. Smell the warm breezes. . .

Nearby, there are fragrant bushes and fruit trees. . .

Notice the white sandy beaches with surfing waves. Touch the sand. . .

Hear the ocean waves as they break on the sandy shore. . .

See a desert scene, and hear the wind as it blows the Joshua trees. . .

See a deserted island with beautiful driftwood on the shores. . .

See rolling green hills. Blend into the landscape around you. . .

See a chain of mountains with snow-covered trees. Experience the snow. . .

*Remember the cold of an icy wind, while you experience
the warmth inside the room. . .*

*Notice tall glaciers in the background, generating streams
of slate grey. . .*

Hear the splashing from a nearby crystal clear waterfall. . .

*Imagine that you can step outside the earth and see your-
self in space. . .*

Feel yourself surrounded by a thousand stars. . .

*Notice the planets all around you. Experience how differ-
ent they are. . .*

See yourself in outer space beyond our galaxy. . .

*Become aware of other galaxies, each one uniquely differ-
ent. . .*

*Experience your own uniqueness and the vastness of the
universe. . .*

You can learn to experience those scenes which are vastly
pleasurable to you by writing them out in your Journal, and then
recording them, slowly, on a tape recorder to allow your creativity
to evolve as you follow the rich imagery described earlier.

The real and the imagined cannot always be separated by the
mind and body. This can be demonstrated by the fantasies and
images which surround human sexuality. Fantasies can be instru-
mental in increasing sexual awareness, and sometimes sexual release. The images which you can produce will give your body the
feelings and experiences as though they were actually taking place.
Try the following exercise by reading the small paragraph below, and
then closing your eyes.

Imagine that you are in your kitchen at home. . .

Go to the refrigerator and take out a lemon. . .

Now, on the cutting board, cut the lemon in two. . .

Now take a big bite out of the lemon. . .

Before you read on, please complete the above exercise, and then answer the following questions:

Was the lemon sweet or sour?
Did your mouth salivate, or could you feel your lips pucker?

However you responded, your body and mind acted as though the lemon was real. This exercise has been used to convince many people that the mind and body do not know the difference between the real and the imagined. In this program, you will learn to use imagery to produce real changes in your life.

As a way of improving your own imagery skills, you can enlarge on the relaxation methods which follow. Additionally, there are many, many good books on imagery, some in the Suggested Readings, which will enhance your imagery ability. Become an expert on which type of imagery relaxes you the deepest. Check yourself to see if you are visual, auditory or kinesthetic. Do you see things mentally, or is your hearing more relaxing to you, or do you feel in your body sensations which produce relaxation for you? Experiment with the following three modes to learn your major system.

We all use either seeing, hearing, or feeling as the predominant method to process information coming in. Using the preferred method for yourself will deepen your imagery experiences:

Visual — seeing mode
Imagine that you are in a room where you lived as a child, and see the furniture, walls and windows. See the toy you loved most, and the bed you slept in. Visualize your parent tucking you in for the night; see the face clearly. See yourself lying in the bed and going to sleep.

Auditory — hearing mode
Hear the sounds in the house where you lived as a child, and imagine that you are in your room playing your favor-

ite music. Hear the singer or orchestra, and the beat of the drums. Hear yourself playing with your favorite toys, and the noises that they make. Imagine that your parent is saying goodnight, and hear what they are saying. Hear the sounds in the house as you begin to drift off into sleep.

Kinesthetic — feeling mode

Imagine that you are at home in your childhood place, and feel the floor in your bedroom, and the sensations of lying in your bed under your favorite cover. Visualize yourself touching and holding your favorite toy. Feel your parent covering you up for the night, and the softness of the kiss. Feel relaxation envelop you as you go to sleep.

If you put these three experiences on a tape, and expand on them using the same mode in each case, you will learn which mode relaxes you the most. We use all the modes all the time, but there is one predominant mode which is particularly our own. Using this mode means we are in synchronization with ourselves. Notice, too, your language; do you mostly say "I see," "I hear" or "I feel" when you are describing something. This, too, will give you some insight into your major representational mode of interacting with your environment.

Scenes of Beauty for Relaxation and to Improve Imagery

Close your eyes, take three slow, deep breaths, and say to yourself, "I am relaxed" each time you breathe.

A Meadow

Nestled at the base of a pine-clad mountain, visualize a lovely meadow. It is spring, and the green carpet of the valley is filled with the brilliant colors of wildflowers. The quiet is enhanced by the gentle sound of a rippling stream, as it flows over the small rocks, as it goes gently by. You can feel the soft breeze on your cheeks, and you feel very, very happy as you watch clouds floating lazily by in the blue, blue sky. You breathe in the pure air and enjoy the serenity around you.

A Beautiful Beach

On a tropical island, imagine a white, sandy beach, with deep blue water and waves breaking gently onto the shore. The sun feels warm and comfortable on your body. In the distance, a bell is slowly chiming a rhythmic melody. You can see birds flying by, and feel the soft wind on your skin. All is well with your world, as you notice the palm trees, the flowers, and fragrant bushes, as you breathe in deeper and deeper, and allow yourself to relax.

A Country Scene

Imagine a country scene from your childhood. Perhaps there were a few peaceful cows wending their way across the valley. The sounds of their lowing mingles with the sound of the wind in the trees. The fields are a patchwork of green, gold and brown, divided by lines of trees or furrows of earth. Gently swelling hills nearby are etched against the sky, and seem to stretch into eternity. You sense the heat from the sun and the warm breeze, as you relax even deeper.

Sui Generis Meditation

Arrange to be in a quiet place where you will not be disturbed for 15 minutes. Sit in a chair with your body and head supported, and eyes closed. Place your legs and your hands comfortably apart. Begin to notice your breathing, and take in four deep breaths, and become aware of how UNIQUE you are. Slowly learn to discover the uniqueness *of each of your body parts. Explore and oxygenate every part of yourself, by using all your senses to see, hear, taste, touch and feel your own unique inner world. Marvel at the intricacy of your own legs, from your toes to the thighs. Then from your fingertips to your shoulders. Then slowly explore the magnificence of your inner body. Lastly, noting each part inside your head. Nowhere in the universe is there another interior exactly like yours.*

Now, locate a spot of light inside yourself. Breathing deeper and deeper, experience that light spreading to your entire body. If you choose the light in your toes, experience it spreading with each breath up your legs, up your arms, through your body and head. Breathe in the light until you are filled with calm, serene and radiant peace. Allow yourself to be filled with your own light, and then repeat over and over the word UNIQUE to give you an appreciation of your self-worth. This silent appreciation of your value as a human being, together with the Sui Generis Meditation, will teach you mastery and self-control in your interpersonal relations. The more firmly you are grounded in your own sense of self, the more accurately you are able to value yourself and others. You are SUI GENERIS.

In imagery, you have the capability of looking deep inside yourself, at any time in your life, and discover a great many things about yourself of which you have been unaware. There are strengths you have not even begun to use yet. You have a self-sufficiency you may not have learned to rely on. For all the things people around you can supply, you can supply those things and much, much more for yourself. Look deep inside yourself and discover your own independence. Examine, too, where it is appropriate to be interdependent, and where you must, for your own integrity, stand alone. Look in the face those things which you fear the most and discover your own courage. Take time to examine what might seem like weaknesses, and discover the strength you have underneath them.

If you have spent much of your life giving in to the wishes of others for fear they will not love you, or will leave you, now is the time to become aware of the high price you might be paying for their love and presence in your life. Examine your relationships as though you were an outside observer, and ask yourself: "If I were not one of those two people, would I stay in that relationship?" Check the alibis you use to defend any poor relationships. Make sure the price you are paying is not too high.

You may discover from this inner search that the relationship you are in is of profound value, and this knowledge will strengthen you. As you show your appreciation to your significant other it will strengthen both of you. There are few things of more value than a truly deep, committed relationship. However, even within such an ideal state, it is necessary to discover yourself as a separate person, and the place to start is deep inside yourself.

Inner Tranquility

You have the capability to discover within yourself a room of tranquility where you can work on all aspects of your life. At a time when you will not be disturbed, get comfortably relaxed, close your eyes, and watching your gentle breathing, let the world outside slip away. Now reach inside yourself to your inner core, and create for yourself a special room, place or space that is uniquely your own. Take all the time you need to arrange this area so that it produces a feeling of peace and comfort within you. Furnish it with natural or manufactured items which will delight you. Bring in the image clearly and strongly. Do nothing else with the space right now, just be aware of how it looks, and know that you can return to it anytime you wish.

Before you return to this area again, I would like you to daydream in a quiet place to discover who and what you would like to have in this space with you. You may choose to remain alone there if you wish. Would you like an electronic calendar, which can be turned to any day, date or time? Put it in there if you wish. Would you like a stage, television or film screen, where you can bring in anyone or anything in the world for you to have conversations with? If you would, put it in your special area. Now take the time to think of what other possessions you would like to have in your special place. Take your time and make it as you wish it to be.

Therapist Within

Inner tranquility in your special area involves your choosing a very, very special person to be your guide. Someone you can dialogue with, talk over your problems with, and help you to make important decisions. When you have your area arranged so that it is perfect for you, choose to go there in imagination, to become deeply relaxed, and to decide who this special person will be who is going to be your guide for life. The person you choose will be the right person for you.

After you have taken all this time to arrange this beautiful place for yourself, it is recommended that you spend time there at least twice a week. Make it a time when you probably won't be disturbed, you know which is the best time for you, and write on your calendar that you will meet with your guide twice a week to discuss matters of importance to you.

You might choose to examine the:

Past	— to reassign value to your life.
Present	— to visualize present opportunities.
Future	— imagine it clearly, and program your life the way you want it to be.

The brain is the greatest healer; give it an opportunity to work for you. When you have a serious problem, do seek professional help. At other times, it is very beneficial to talk to the therapist within.

When you are alone, experience this person in your mind as clearly as you can and use the methods in this book to work on your current issues.

Contacting your deeper resources can be accomplished by relaxing comfortably and closing your eyes and guiding yourself through the following experience:

Start by visualizing a meadow, in full detail, with all of your senses, and then notice a pathway leading to a quiet blue lake. Become aware that you can swim under the clear water, and swim for a while to see if there is anyone or anything of interest to you in the water. If there is anyone there, invite them to come to the shore with you, and return to the meadow. Notice in the distance that there is a mountain where you can slowly wend your way up to the top, very comfortably taking a gentle pathway, or ascend directly to the top of the mountain. When you arrive there, become aware of all the scenery at the top, the breathtaking view, the clarity of the air, and notice that there is someone there who wants to speak with you.

Ask the person whatever special question seems right to you at that moment; such as, "What is it I need in my life right now?" and listen carefully to what your special guide tells you. When you have dialogued long enough, ask the person for a gift. Thank them for the gift and bring it back with you down the mountainside to the meadow. Examine the gift carefully, and ask yourself, "What does this mean in my life right now?" A gift from your inner self is an important symbol of something which would enhance your life. Whatever it symbolizes, take the time to look for it in the real world. If it was a flower, you might choose a painting of it, or a gold flower to represent it to wear on a chain, or fresh flowers. Whatever seems to represent the

gift to you is all that you need to remember that you have
that particular capacity within you. Keep the symbol as an
important message from your inner self.

Giving yourself creative gifts from your own inner self can be achieved by:

1. Imagining a golden line between yourself and other people. Each time you meet a new person, say to yourself, "Without question, we like each other," and a golden line will form.
2. Wear a "zapping machine" on your wrist, like an invisible watch. When anyone is mean to you, you can zap them, and as far as you are concerned, they will disappear until they stop being mean.
3. Give yourself the knowledge that you need never be without a friend, because no matter what happens, you will always have yourself as a friend.
4. Your own inner transformation can be your gift from YOU to YOU.
5. What you have as gifts today are the seeds of what you can become tomorrow, and the planting time is now.

Creativity

With its over-developed skills, the left brain has difficulty allowing the right brain to operate on a conscious level. In order to forge a more satisfying life, you must learn the ability to use right-hemispheric skills using imagery and creativity. Achieving excellence for yourself can be done imaginatively by changing perspectives of the world by:

●   Picking a different area of competence than your own, and choose a model in that field, and integrate those features into your personality.

- Look at other cultures and pick a personality from them, whether from the past or present; i.e., a doctor, sailor or lawyer, and teach yourself to see life from that view.
- The following year, and every year thereafter, choose another personality and let that personality benefit your own.
- Practice being an alien and view the world as he might.
- Imagine that you are a child again, and experience the delight of doing such things as driving a car, or staying up late, or any of the things an adult does.
- Create your own model of excellence. Your inner mind knows a great deal, and if you will spend time listening to yourself, you will learn what is right for you.

You have far greater capabilities than you give yourself credit for, and excellence is within your grasp; all you have to do is to reach within and contact the source of your own creativity.

Further imagery exercises follow:

Sunrise and Sunset

Close your eyes, uncross your arms and legs, deeply relax against what is supporting you. Breathing in. . . . Breathing out. . . . Breathing in. . . . Breathing out. . . .

Imagine you are slowly waking up from a restful sleep. It is early morning and you can hear the wild birds singing. In the distance, across the lake and behind the mountains, you can see the early morning sun begin to rise.

As the dawn breaks, you can see brilliant rays of sunshine reflecting from the white clouds above. The sun gets brighter and brighter as it rises higher and higher in the sky.

You feel the warmth increase as the sun moves into the noonday sky. You bask in the warmth of the long and lazy, relaxing afternoon that seems to last an eternity.

As the sun starts to settle low in the evening sky, it forms a pathway of gold across the lake. Slowly it slips behind the mountains reflecting a brilliant red from the clouds.

The colors change to amber, purple and gold, and you are filled with happiness. The entire earth is wrapped in beauty, creating happy thoughts of the ending of a perfect day.

You have within your memory many perfect images. To become your own imagery specialist, you can relax by running the beauty of these experiences across your mind for deeper and deeper periods of relaxation.

Planet Pluto

Imagine that you are on the furthest planet, Pluto, and that it is full of hundreds of colors that you have never seen before. What color would you make familiar things, and what new colors can you invent for unfamiliar things. Changing the color of anything changes its nature; for example, a red, white and green flag would be a different way of seeing the Stars and Stripes.

Kaleidoscope (From the Greek — Beautiful form)

Imagine the color pink, a pale baby pink, becoming a medium pink, and developing into a deep, deep rose.
Now green, a pale spring green, changing to a middle shade of green, and becoming a deep kelly green.
Imagine a light shade of orange, turning to a medium shade of orange, into a deep, deep shade of bronze.
Now a pale, baby blue turns into a medium shade of blue, becoming a deep indigo blue.
Then a light shade of red, changing to a medium shade of

red, and becoming a brilliant shade of crimson.

Now a pale, pale white, changing to a medium shade of white, and becoming a brilliant, dazzling white.

Imagine a pale daffodil yellow, changing to a medium yellow, and becoming a deep, deep gold.

Now a pale shade of lavender, changing to a medium shade of purple, and becoming a deep royal purple.

Now imagine a kaleidoscope of color, where all the beautiful forms are present, from the palest shades on the palette of colors to medium shades of colors, developing into the deepest, most brilliant jewel tones.

This is a form of beauty which is always there for your delight and, at any time, you can close your eyes and deeply relax while watching the beauty evolve to evoke deep relaxation.

Personality color

Now choose a color to represent your personality, and imagine the color you have chosen. Let it range from the palest shade (almost a pale white) to the deepest shade (almost an inky black). In acknowledging only one end of the spectrum, the other end is cut out. However, in recognizing the full spectrum of color within your personality, you can choose to live in the vibrant area. You can leave the insipid shade, acknowledge the uncomfortable-for-living shades, and choose to be in full contact with your life energy and creativity expressed by the vibrant shade which is YOU.

Beyond the Galaxies

Go to the deepest level of relaxation you can achieve by your favorite means, and concentrate on your breathing. This experience is to permit you to transcend your body, and may create the feeling you might be striving for in meditation or relaxation. Slowly tape the following:

Imagine that you are sitting in a chair, or lying in bed, and see yourself clearly. Now stand outside your body, and look at yourself. See every detail of your face and body, and the surroundings in the room. Then float up to the ceiling and look at yourself below. Now float up on the roof, and see the house below. Look at the outside of your home, and allow yourself to float, safely, even higher. See the whole town below you, and then the surrounding towns. Now see the entire state, and the surrounding states. Then see the whole of the country, and the oceans surrounding it. Going higher to see all the countries near yours, and the oceans between them.

Become aware that you can float outside the earth's atmosphere, and look across at the full beauty of the slowly rotating earth. Just like the view astronauts see, you marvel at the sight. You float past all the other planets and stars until you have passed Pluto, the furthest planet. Soon you are outside our galaxy, and you can see all the other galaxies in the universe. You experience powerful emotions as you witness your universe. Now it is time to enter the Milky Way, to go past Pluto and all the other planets and stars, until you are again approaching earth. As you enter earth's atmosphere, down below you can see your country, and the state you live in, and pretty soon, your own hometown. Nearby is the house you live in, and you slip into your room. You recognize your body and can feel it as you slip inside. You feel all your bodily sensations as you gently, slowly return to the room.

Magic Magnet

Use your favorite method of deep relaxation, and concentrate-on your breathing, and become aware of the difference in your body as you inhale. . .and as you exhale. . .

Now imagine that you are able to bring together in your forehead all your unwanted emotions. . . . Gently touch your forehead in a circle, going round and round with your fingers. Imagine that you can bring together, all in one place in your forehead, all your fear, anxiety, tension and pain. . . all your disappointments, unhappiness and sorrow. . . . All the emotions you would like erased from your life.

Now that you have brought all of these tensions into one place, I would like you to imagine that by magic you have turned them into a magnetizable force. At your feet is a very large magnet. . .visualize, hear, touch and sense it clearly. Imagine that you can feel the magnet drawing away every unwanted emotion. Beginning with your head, feel the emotions draining down through your face. . . jaw . . . neck and shoulders. . . . Now your arms and fingers. Notice that the magnet is draining all the emotions out of your neck and shoulders and down your chest. . . waist, and lower body. Now from your upper, middle and lower spine. . . Your thighs, knees, calves and legs are draining, as are your ankles, feet and toes. . . .

Take a moment to make sure that your body is fully drained, and that all of your body feels light, calm, relaxed and wonderful. Look at the magnet until it disappears into the void, taking with it all the unwanted emotions. Experience them traveling far, far away from you. Disappearing out of sight, sound and touch, completely out of your experience.

Now imagine, after the magnet has disappeared completely, that you are lying somewhere very, very comfortable. . . . Overhead there is a warm, glowing light. You can feel this warmth and comfort from the light all over your body. . . . This light is filling you with all the emotions you want in your life: comfort, security, happi-

ness, independence, and love, plus strength, satisfaction and deep relationships. Now take a moment to include any emotion that you especially feel you need inside.

You can now feel your body filling up with these positive and powerful emotions, from your toes, feet, legs, up through your lower body, waist, chest and shoulders. . . Your fingers, hands, and arms are slowly filling with this warm feeling. . . Your neck, face and head slowly fill with this great feeling. You feel these positive emotions filling your whole body completely with each breath you breathe.

Any time you want to you can bring together any thoughts which are troubling you, and gather them gently into one place in your forehead, and feel the magnetic pull as they are drained out of your body. Then gently allow your body to be filled with all the positive emotions that you wish.

Colorful Growth

Allow yourself to float on a cloud, and experience pleasant feelings in your body as you allow yourself to drift across the sky. As you become aware of your breathing, you relax even deeper and deeper. You are safe, relaxed and comfortable, and sounds drift away as your body becomes heavy and warm, relaxed and refreshed, as you drift through space, and relax.

And now, as you relax further, I want you to imagine that you are breathing in crystal clean air, and breathing out the color:

Black:　　*Imagine that black represents all the tension, stress and strain in your life, and each breath out releases it and washes it away. In/Out. . . In/Out. . .In/Out. Until there is no trace of black left. . .*

Red: And as you breathe out this time, experience the color red, which might represent all the hot emotions: anger, hostility, rage, resentment and fear. Breathing in crystal clean air, and breathing out any hot emotions until they are drained completely away. In/Out . . . In/Out. . . In/Out.

Purple: And now breathing out the color purple, and imagining that the color purple is all the pain, illness or negative emotions that you do not need to hold in your muscles. Let them all drain out, as you breathe In/Out. . . In/Out. . . In/Out.

Snow White: Imagine that as you relax even further that you are breathing out the color white, an icy whiteness, which represents all the cold emotions: indifference, coldness, aloofness and alienation. As you breathe in good air, and breathe out these cold emotions, your body will experience warmth and relaxation, as you breathe In/Out. . . In/Out. . . In/Out.

Let all those images disappear, and now change your breathing pattern by breathing in the following colors:

Blue: Breathe in the color blue: the blue of the sky, the ocean of clear blue water, fills you up with calmness, tranquility and peace. Just breathing in the color blue, as you breathe In/Out. . . In/Out. . . In/Out.

Green: And now the color green is being breathed in, the color of new growth. Feel yourself grow as you sprout out like a tree whose leaves are uncurling, and whose branches are

52

growing and reaching upwards to the sky. Growing and growing to your fullest potential, as you breathe in green, and fill your body with positive thoughts and images about yourself and your capabilities. In/Out. . . In/Out. . . In/Out.

Yellow: *You experience now the color yellow, as it is breathed into your body, as the yellow warmth of the sun, the sand, and the brightness of yellow flowers — daffodils, tulips and yellow chrysanthemums. All this warmth and happiness is being breathed into your body as you experience the color yellow. In/Out. . . In/Out. . . In/Out.*

Gold: *And the color turns to gold, a warm and mellow gold, and you experience feelings of ripeness and warmth, as you breathe in the color gold. There is a sense of security, happiness and growth as you allow yourself to smile as you fill yourself with golden joy, as you breathe In/Out. . .In/Out. . . In/Out*

Rub together two fingers and know that in your busy life, at any time in the day, you can re-experience this feeling by putting your two fingers together and breathing in the color gold.

Growth Imagery

Humans go through the same seasons as flowers, plants and trees do. Sometimes you may have to lie dormant and withdrawn, and be less energetic while you are building new structures for growth in the future. Relax, and listen intently to your tape of this:

Right now it is spring. It is the end of winter where you have been resting, and now you are in the ground where it is dark and cool. I want you to imagine that you are a seed or bulb in the ground. Decide now what kind of flower or fruit you will become. . . Feel the darkness surrounding you, and the cool moistness of the earth. You become aware that this is the time for growing, and you can feel the earth becoming warmer from the sun. There is a feeling of light and warmth. Rain is gently providing moisture and life as it gently falls all around you. The sun is providing photosynthesis and warmth. . . Feel yourself beginning to grow. . . Feel the spring air as you thrust your way up through the ground. Be aware of the changes in your own organism as you grow and grow.

Notice that you are becoming the kind of flower or fruit that you chose to be. First, look at your shape, size, color and texture. . . Be aware of the changes in your own organism as you grow and grow. . . First, you are leaves and blossoms, and perhaps later delicious fruit. Is there a scent from your blossoms floating in the wind? Are you quiet or do you make sounds when the wind blows through you? Are bees humming happily around your petals and leaves? Remember the qualities of the flower or fruit that you were experiencing. This is a new period of life and growth.

LEVEL 5: **PRIMARY LEVEL II**

Powerful Emotions

Moving to different levels of thinking has no particular sequence, the level changes with the current life situation you are in. You will be exercising your flexibility by operating on the level which is required by each life situation. The following levels are best incorporated into your personality as you have need of them:

Compassion	–	Learning to forgive
Courage	–	Discovering your inner strengths
Desensitization	–	To pain and loss
Grieving	–	Reinvesting in life
Pain	–	Discovering comfort

A great deal of emotional pain can be created by overlooking the choices which are open to you for compassion and courage. To some painful events it is necessary to learn desensitization, which is very effective in overcoming fears and phobias. Cultivating your strengths to overcome discomfort is worth the effort to be pain free. Continue to use these levels as necessary to maximize your comfort and happiness.

Compassion Level

The moment you become aware that you are in a blaming mode, either of yourself or other people, you can mentally occupy a higher level in the building of your personality. This can be done by immediately forgiving those involved and going on with healthier thoughts. When you notice that your thoughts are in chaos, or require switching from negative to positive evaluations of the situation, immediately visualize yourself forgiving yourself and/or others. Change the situation if you can and, if you cannot, mentally visualize yourself ascending to a higher level of brain activity by stopping the endless tape in your head, and forgiving totally. When you do this, experience the relief in your body. Treat yourself as you would treat a dear friend who had transgressed, and be kind to yourself.

Suggested sentences to yourself on the compassion level might be:

1. I did the very best I could.
2. I am worthy of forgiveness and so is my friend.
3. Positive emotions are my allies.
4. The greatest gift I can give myself and others is forgiveness.
5. What happened was then, and this is now; now I can forgive.

Imagine your younger self, who perhaps is overwhelmed with what happened in the past, and take the older you back there. Tell your younger self that you can handle the situation now. In imagination dialogue together, find out what your younger self needs and wants, and explain how, now that you are older, you can take care of that younger self. Forgive yourself totally — if you won't, then who will? Learn to befriend yourself constantly on the compassion level.

There are some wrongs which can never be righted. Murderous rage and resentment about those wrongs are held in the body muscles

56

as tension. This creates physical and emotional pain, and changing this situation is most desirable. No matter how deep the scars, nor how tight the muscle tension, actual physical and emotional relief can be experienced by forgiving on a grand scale. Avoid holding on to *any part* of your resentment. Let go by saying to yourself, "I forgive totally" and really mean it. You are doing this for yourself, not for the other person. You are the one being hurt by the intensity of your feelings. You are also the one who will benefit most by being compassionate. You may or may not choose to tell anyone about this forgiveness. Just feel in your own body deeply forgiving the individual, and experience the relief of letting go of the pain. When you have mastered one major area of compassion, an excellent idea is to totally forgive anyone else who has ever harmed you. The key to your comfort is forgiveness.

The brain can, with lightning speed, understand comprehensive data, and you can reprogram yourself to forgive all those who have hurt you, and forgive yourself, in a very short time. Several suggestions for doing this follow. It sometimes happens that the far reaches of the brain take a long time to get the message you are sending it. As you become aware that parts of your brain have not yet received the message, repeat the processes of totally forgiving and therapeutically forgetting. You will achieve a sense of peace and tranquility which will radiate to many areas of your day. In a major way, you can invigorate your life and change your personality by recognizing how your brain interacts physically, physiologically and psychologically when you adopt a compassionate level of operating.

The releasing factors in the brain respond to your senses and thoughts, and if your thoughts are filled with resentment, rage and pain, stress hormones will be released into your bloodstream. The afferent responses from the senses to the brain, which trigger these hormones, are under your direct control. If the afferent responses from thinking are positive, only sufficient hormones will be released to provide excitement and motivation. If the thinking is negative, you, personally, turn on the switch to the releasing of stress hormones. The way you think determines the emotions you experience, and you can control your emotions by changing your thinking. This in turn can reduce stress.

It is apparent from your physiological makeup, which responds to your psychological reactions, that learning to deal with how you think about the people in your life will enable you to operate in the comfort zone. This is the way in which forgiving yourself and others pays great personal dividends. Letting go of resentment, rage and pain, by forgiving and forgetting, frees up your creative energy. Not releasing stress hormones in your body leaves your body free to work on its immunological tasks. Your immunity from disease frequently determines your lifespan, and preserving its accurate functioning can be critical to life.

A very strong suggestion for controlling negative thoughts is practice of compassion towards yourself and all other people you have not previously forgiven. In your Journal, and in your thinking, please record:

I, (YOUR FULL NAME) TOTALLY FORGIVE MYSELF AND ALL OTHERS, AND THERAPEUTICALLY FORGET WHAT NEEDS TO BE FORGOTTEN.

Using imagery, in a relaxed state, visualize the words in full color. Hear the words as you say them silently, or put them to music inside yourself. Feel the words throughout the whole of your body, as you experience total forgiveness to yourself and everybody you need to forgive. Conjure up a smell which will remind you of this experience, perhaps a pink rose, or mountain pine tree, or any smell which delights you. The more total you can make this experience, the more benefit you will derive from it.

Keep, as a tape, the refrain of forgiveness to yourself and others and practice putting the therapeutic forgetting into action by stopping any thoughts which negate totally forgiving. In time you may only need to remember your decision to totally forgive, and therapeutically forget to reinstigate yourself on the compassion level. You are not doing this for the benefit of anyone else, although it appears that others might benefit from your changed thinking. You are doing it for yourself, to increase your mastery and self-control of your internal and external environment.

Motivating yourself to operate on the compassion level gives you back your own power which you may have inadvertently given away to the authority of parents, schools, churches, or others. You are choosing to be the authority on how you will deal with yourself and other people in selecting a compassionate world view. In totally forgiving and therapeutically forgetting, there may or may not be transfer of this information to others involved, or reconcilation with them. You may choose to do both those things or neither. You are striving to operate your life on a higher level with compassionate thinking, and the behavior which follows will be designed to enhance your intra-and-interpersonal relationships as appropriate for YOU.

Courage Level

Each situation you are faced with, where you need to overcome fear, presents you with an opportunity to seek your own strengths, and will enable you to review life events from a broader perspective. Courageous thinking opens up avenues that anxious or fearful thinking blocks out. You can increase your number of life options by getting in touch with your own courage.

Imagining yourself on this level means searching within and keeping on when the odds seem to be against you. Perserverance pays even when you don't fully succeed because you know that you gave it your best effort. Anxiety can distort thinking so that reducing it by changing your thought patterns is beneficial. For example, anytime when anxiety or fear are high and you have not yet figured out a strategy for turning the situation into a challenge mentally, get in touch with your own courage level. You may choose to view the fear as a burden which is dragging you under and, in imagery, you may decide to put the burden down in order to free you to act creatively and meet the current challenge. Place the fear on a train, in imagery, and let the train travel to the far reaches of the world. Mentally see yourself leaving any negative emotions behind and move to the courage level.

Anxiety has brought many people into therapy, and this has the merit of being the incentive they needed to make some important changes in their lives and move on in a way that might not have been possible without therapy. Therapy can put people in touch with their own courage when the fear seems insurmountable. However, there is much you can do to put youself in touch with your own courage.

There may be within you a small child who needs your love and support now that you are an adult. As a child, you may have cared for everyone else but not yourself. Now is the time to nurture yourself. Although you may have made a lot of mistakes, you also made many, many good decisions. Give yourself credit for those. Stop beating yourself mercilessly about the past; you were probably not responsible for what happened and even if you were, you did the best you could with the knowledge you had at the time. Instead of examining what is wrong with your life, look at what is right. Now you are aware of the inner selves, you have many choices you can make to help your inner child grow up. Before using your subconscious, you only had access to 10% of your brain; now you have access to the rest of the 90% from your work with meditation and other skills.

You can retrieve the best of your own childhood and share it with your children. If your inner child was afraid of the dark, give the child a light in the present to represent security. Give your child a magic treasure box from your adult world where she can enjoy the things you have today. Learn to understand what the inner you wants and learn to give it to her. Trust your inner guide, make friends with your inner child and mature her. What you left undone in the past gives you the opportunity to do something good in the future. Many of your inner child's successes brought you to where you are today.

Much of what frightens us as adults is based on childhood fears and one way to deal with intimidation from authority figures from our past is to practice the Balloon Method and experience your own power.

Balloon Method

If you are in a situation where you feel intimidated by someone else, right now imagine the first time that you began to feel the intimidation. If it is an office, at what time do you begin to feel the fear and how do you visualize the person? What do they look like, sound like, and what does it feel like for you? Once you have a clear picture of when the intimidation begins, imagine that you can reduce them in size. At the same time, imagine that you can make a balloon of yourself. Inhale and blow yourself up and as you do, notice that the other person gets smaller and smaller. Any time you feel intimidated by someone else, close your eyes, imagine that you are a balloon and breathe in deeply and blow yourself up larger and larger until you are towering over the person who is attempting to intimidate you. Make yourself as large as you need to be to be free of fear.

Animal strength

In a relaxed state, close your eyes, and imagine that you have inside yourself a very strong animal who can provide you with all the courage you need to deal with anything that makes you fearful. Can you visualize yourself as a lion, tiger or mountain ram? Look inside yourself to discover an animal to represent your courage. When you locate him, make the animal real by going out and purchasing a toy model, picture or charm, and keep it where you can see it. This will remind you that you can use these characteristics to deal with fear and display your courage.

You may be familiar with the Morton Hunt story, "The Lesson of the Cliff," in which he describes four fearful events in his life: first as an 8-year-old being stuck on a cliff, too paralyzed with fear to go up or go down; the second as a pilot flying over enemy territory; the third the terror of uncertainty about writing a book he had a contract for; and finally, separation from his wife and children. After a very moving description of deep human fear in these events, Morton takes the reader back to the first time when, fatigued and stupified, he clung to the cliff face as the sun went down. His description of what happened then contained the key to his own courage. His father came and guided him down off the cliff by shining a flashlight to show him where to put his feet, and telling him to do it *one step at a time*. This, too, reflects the same idea used by Alcoholics Anonymous — one day at a time. Morton learned this as a young child, and applied it since then to all the other life situations he wrote about.

You, too, can take this simple lesson from Morton Hunt and many others of tackling frightening prospects in small segments, one step at a time. There is nothing you cannot achieve which requires courage that cannot be conquered one step at a time. No matter how great the task, how fearful, how hazardous, the human spirit can conquer most tasks in small increments. You can provide safety and courage for yourself *in the present moment* of what you need to do to accomplish a terrifying task by staying present in this small segment of time and performing one small part of the task. You can use Morton, or someone similar from your readings or life, as a model for courage. What can be done by each one of us to overcome our fears lights the way for others to experience their own courage.

Desensitized Level

This level will teach you desensitization and how to truly let go of hurt and pain from loss. To be rejected or unloved by someone you care for elicits hatred and rage, and often triggers previous rejection experiences. As long as you remain stuck in these negative emotions, you are emotionally tied to the loss. Learning to cultivate a neutral position of true indifference will take away the other's ability to hurt you. As long as you "hang on" to the negative thoughts and feelings about the loss, you cannot reinvest your feelings in something new. Cultivating neutral feelings of indifference will help you to let go of the negative emotions.

A variation of Wolpe's method of systematic desensitization is recommended using a tape and tape recorder. To desensitize yourself to the rejection trauma, write out a list of 10 to 15 sentences describing what is painful to you about the loss. Then make a hierarchy, ranking the sentences from least to most painful. Put each sentence on tape with a 30 second pause between each one. In the loss of a love relationship, your list might read:

1. We will not spend pleasant times together.
2. I will not be held or kissed by _____
3. There will be no sex with _____
4. There will be no loving support from _____
5. This situation will not change.
6. Our time together is over.
7. Our plans will not be reached.
8. I am not loved by _____
9. I will be alone for some time.
10. _____ may be with someone else.

When you have completed your hierarchy of sentences, put them on a tape with pauses in between and begin to practice your deepest relaxation method. Take yourself mentally to a safe place, on the beach, in a forest, or on a mountain top, and counting backwards, allow yourself to reach your deepest level of relaxation. Your tape should be placed where you can easily reach it for stopping and starting it. Begin by listening to *one* sentence at a time, switching off the tape each time you cannot maintain your state of relaxation. When you feel alarmed, stop the recorder and relax yourself again, and then commence listening to the sentences again. Each time you become tense, restart at the beginning sentence until you can listen to the complete hierarchy while remaining relaxed. This method can be used for any list of fears or anxieties. When you can stay relaxed listening to the items which previously bothered you, you will notice a very surprising thing; the relaxation will generalize to the same *real life* situations. For example, once you can conquer and accept the fact in imagery that the person you have lost will be with someone else, you will be able to tolerate it in your everyday life. A state of tension cannot exist where there is a state of relaxation, and providing a state of relaxation and coupling it with previously tense situations will enable you to maintain relaxation and neutral feelings when you are in the same situations in real life.

A patient was able to overcome her fear of being held up at the point of a gun on her job by working with systematic desensitization for six visits. You can desensitize yourself to all but very traumatic life events, which would require a therapist's help, by using your own skill at desensitization.

Grieving Level

No matter how painful, grieving must be processed in order to reinvest your emotions in someone or something else and to reconnect yourself to life and living. For healthy living, it is absolutely necessary to grieve effectively. Emotions such as painful loss cannot be cut off by pretending they don't exist. Cutting off negative emotions causes loss of positive emotions and the result is a feeling of deadness. Grieving may be, for example, for a person, pet or job. For easier discussion, death of a person has been used in this section, but the process is the same to work with feelings of loss and abandonment. This might be done by:

1. Permitting the tears to flow for five or ten minutes each

day; to cry as hard as you can for what was lost. Then wash your face, and go on with your day.

2. Experience your feelings of anger, sadness and pain at being left without letting it spoil the whole day.

3. Review all your experiences with the deceased, good or bad, as though you were watching a film in an empty theatre.

4. In privacy, dialogue in imagery with the deceased and say all the things you may never have had the chance to say.

5. Examine your own mortality. It will help you to appreciate and value each day of your own life.

6. Talk to a trusted friend about the person you loved and lost.

7. Give your loved person another life by taking the qualities you learned from that person and passing them on to your children and their children, so that, in some way, later generations will know you and your loved one.

As long as you live, the person you lost will never die. That person will live in your memory as long as you exist and in a healthy manner, with time, you will be able to appreciate all the positive aspects of the relationship. In time, you may become aware that in the eye of every catastrophe there is the seed of a miracle. Each day, even though exhausted by the energy drain from the loss, remind yourself that you must go one more mile for the sake of others who love you.

Allow the sadness to pass through you. In a relaxed state, allow your breathing to support you and be aware that for some people the person they have lost seems to hang around as long as they need them. It may be that they appear in a relaxed reverie, or a dream, or in some fashion of sensing that the person is still there when you need them and is still looking after your needs and caring for you. It seems that our immortality is tied up in the best qualities that we take from those we have loved and pass them on to our grandchildren, or those who come after us.

There might have been a time when the grief was so strong that you closed the door because you had to, but now you have another choice to open the door and let in a crack of light. Allow yourself the luxury of sitting close to nature and seeing the cycle of the seasons. A tree that appeared dead, or a bulb that shows no growth, suddenly bursts into life and is reborn. Surely if that occurs in plant life, there is some sense to a point of view that it happens in human life. Take comfort from the thought.

Close your eyes and take three deep breaths. Concentrate on your breathing and naturally float into a deeper center of calmness within you. Imagine that you are sitting in a very comfortable chair in a room where you are calm, safe and relaxed. In front of you is a holograph which can bring anyone or anything into the room in three-dimension. Now use that holograph to bring in someone that you are grieving for. Allow the person to be there in totality. See their face and body and hear their voice. Experience the touch of their hands and allow that touch to comfort you. Get in touch with all the feelings of loss and helplessness and allow the person to comfort you. Talk to the person and let them know how you feel. The more you are able to experience your feelings in your body, the more relief you will have later.

All the pain from the past is held in tension in your body and the more you drain away the pain, the more energy you will release. You can learn to let go of the pain and get in touch with all the fine qualities of the person that still remain to remind you of them.

Take out the photographs and the letters and see them more clearly and hear more surely what the person was saying who wrote them. Learn to be grateful for the treasures you have from the past and use them to help you to find strength in the future. To grieve is healthy, and you will find that with time there is healing and you can let the sadness dissolve. Because you are still alive, you know that there is still work for you to do. There are people who need you. You know that you have the courage and the spirit to learn from your tragedy. It will give you an understanding of the pain that others suffer and when it is needed, you will be able to give comfort to someone else. For now, in case there is no one there who can provide you the comfort you need, provide it for youself in a caring, thoughtful manner. Your job is to discover what is the task life now has for you and how best might you prepare yourself to do it.

In adjusting to divorce, separation and loss, it often seems that just when a person believes that a reasonable adjustment has been made, more pain is experienced. Even though the brain thinks with lightning speed, it does not seem to get messages to every part of it at the same time. In loss, for example, you know on many levels that the person is no longer there but on other levels of your brain, you find yourself thinking as though the loss had not occurred. You may have experienced this phenomena which lets you know that some parts of your brain are having difficulty accepting what has happened.

Just when you start to believe that you have adjusted to the divorce, separation or loss, you may find yourself grieving anew. Be aware that this is because the information is only now reaching the deeper recesses of your brain. Allow time for this to happen; it is part of what is needed for adjustment to the loss. A benevolent mechanism seems to operate that permits into comprehension only a bearable amount of pain. As you adjust gradually to the loss, you accumulate the strength to bear the full pain. After the grieving period, you will find relief. Support and comfort yourself in every way you can, knowing that with time the deeper brain recesses will get the full message when you are in a position where you can deal with it.

In a lifetime, there are many painful experiences which must be handled; allowing the more positive emotions to emerge brings strength and courage. Allow the pleasant times to emerge, separating them from your grief and welcoming happiness as each isolated event occurs. These islands of pleasant experiences can form a firm foundation on which to reinvest yourself in living.

Pain Level

Imagery is very effective for pain and these exercises will help you to come up to the comfort level:

Helium Balloon:

Imagine that all the pain in your body is liquid and that you have faucets on your fingers and toes which are connected to pipes. The pipes lead to a helium balloon. Imagine that the pain and all the liquid is slowly draining out of your body through the pipes into the helium balloon. When the basket is full, disconnect the pipes, and imagine that the helium balloon floats higher and higher into the sky, far, far away, until it reaches outer space and disintegrates.

Five to Zero:

Imagine, with your eyes closed, that you can see the number 5 and let it dissolve; then the number 4, 3, 2, and 1, letting each number dissolve slowly until you can see the number 0. Into this zero, imagine that you have placed all the pain and see yourself walking away from the pain.

Another Room:

Imagine that you are sitting on a chair and as you experience the pain, imagine that you can walk into another room and leave the pain behind.

Train Imagery:

Take all the pain you are feeling and in imagination, see yourself wrapping it in a box and taking it to the train station. Put the package on the train and see the train slowly disappearing from sight, taking all the pain with it.

A lovely woman in her seventies was discussing pain and the fact that as a younger woman she did not have the skills from this book. She has since learned to deal with the traumatic loss of her son by using imagery skills and meditation. Her home was vandalized and she is faced with setting up another home, as well as dealing with an operation and back injury. She uses the helium balloon method of draining pain from her body and looks at her life one step at a time. She is able to tackle major tasks by self-control of her pain. Her greatest success story recently was her ability to quit smoking after forty years. This was achieved after only two sessions in the writer's *Habit Busters* program.

A young woman in her thirties was dealing with the pain of a ten year relationship ending and her desire to continue living was being strongly tested at each painful experience of contact with her lover. Using imagery methods, she was able to overcome the pain of loss − which had re-evoked her father's suicide loss − and reinvest her emotions in other friends and her work. She courageously did the hard work involved in dealing with pain in her life.

Pain can be on a physical or psychological level and, with your doctor's approval, you can work with imagery to reduce it. Using relaxation techniques, your muscles can learn to relax and not go into spasms which cause more pain. Imagining your veins expanding, vasodilation, allows the blood to flow freely to heal where required. Where there is emotional tension and pain, it can be reduced by imagery of calm and serene states. You will be pleased with the pain control you can learn to master when you focus intently on producing a relaxed state. Give yourself the opportunity to reduce unnecessary pain by diligently practicing your exercises daily to comfortably handle your powerful emotions.

Powerful Emotions

You have now examined some very powerful emotions: compassion, courage, grief and pain, and you have learned desensitization to pain and loss. Some people choose not to deal with these emotions and spend an enormous amount of time and energy denying their true feelings. Not dealing with them as they occur means that you later have to deal with a much greater accumulation of pain. The only way out of a painful situation is to go through it, dealing with the emotional pain and learning how to reinvest your positive emotions in other areas.

LEVEL 6: **INTERMEDIATE LEVEL I**

Mastery of Emotions

Proceeding with strengthening your ability of successful self-control and mastery continues with additional skills:

Affirmations	– choosing to come from abundance
Humor	– enriching your life with laughter
Happiness and power	– releasing unhappiness and helplessness
Love	– increasing your capacity for joy
Mastery	– enhancing self-control
Philosophy	– improving your daily living
Pleasure	– producing enriched experiences
Self-esteem	– raising your self-esteem

Affirmations are written confirmations of what you strongly desire. Humor is an excellent stress reliever, enriches daily living and puts you in touch with your happinesss and power. As you learn mastery over your philosophy, you can control your life more effectively. You owe it to yourself to experience increased pleasure and enhanced self-esteem. Plan to include all of the following levels into your personality structure:

Affirmations

Creative affirmations can be drafted in your Journal and later written down on a card to be read every day. Begin by deciding whether you are coming from abundance or scarcity. If you come from scarcity, you will believe that there is not enough love, success and happiness in the world for everyone, and you will not share what you have. If you come from abundance, you will believe that there is enough love, success and happiness to go around, and you will find ways to share your abundance.

Right now, choose to come from abundance by seeing that you live in an unlimited universe and you have the ability to produce what you want in life. All that is required is that you learn to focus your energies on whatever it is you want to get. Focusing can be done by writing out affirmations stating what you want from life. Look at your short-term goals and what the long-term result will be. Then write your affirmations as though they already existed. Choose three sentences, similar to the examples written, which are correct for you under these headings:

1. What you are:	*I am glad to be alive and love my life.*
	I am powerful and can handle life's challenges.
	I am joyous and happy and share my life with others.
2. What you can do:	*I can forget the past, live in the present and enjoy the future.*
	I can rise to great heights and become whatever I choose.
	I can take responsibility for all that happens to me.
3. What you will:	*I will succeed in all that I do in life.*

*I will radiate confidence and be
creative and happy.
I will facilitate my own dreams
coming true.*

Focusing on your daily affirmations releases energy, overcomes self-imposed limitations and unleashes your creativity. Keep your card where you can read it daily.

A friend of mine started her own business and needed to promote it by going out to various businesses to describe her work and what she could offer these companies. She had read about making up a commercial about herself and reading it just before she went into the office. So she wrote on a 3x5 card some things about herself and considered herself as an important, a really important woman who thought big about everything. She wrote that she had creative skills and ability to do outstanding work in her business. She noted that she had lots of drive and that nothing could stop her if she would let her enthusiasm show through.

At the end of the "commercial" on herself, she wrote that she looked and felt good. She wrote that she was a great woman yesterday, and was going to be an even greater person today and tomorrow. She told herself to go forward to success; that if anybody could do it, she could. The affirmations she chose to write on the other side of her card included:

*I have the power to deal with all of my life.
The greatest gift I can give myself and others is my own
    inner transformation.
I have a service to offer that this company needs.
I can rise to great heights and become what I choose.
I will radiate confidence, be creative, and happy.*

From the commercial and affirmations, she was able to go into the offices and present her business skills. You can write a commercial about yourself and choose some of the affirmations given, or create your own. Where you have used your own creativity to design affirmations that suit you particularly, you have strengthened your ability to increase your self-esteem and self-acceptance. Go to it. . . if anyone can do it, YOU can.

Cultivating Humor

Creative thinking involves learning to view things humorously. Humor is a valuable human resource, and a humorous attitude can be practiced for handling interpersonal relationships, approaching your goals, and defusing potentially awkward situations. Thinking humorously can increase your self-confidence and add zest to your life as an important natural resource. Humorous thinking can be used to solve problems and become a positive force in your life. You can learn to switch on your humor and give it to others as a bonus.

When you use your creative thinking power to see humor in life situations, people will enjoy your fun-filled spirit and the energy your laughter generates. Learning to laugh at yourself defuses painful experiences and helps you to minimize matters of minor importance. Developing a new perspective on events gives emotional balance. Projecting a lighthearted, good-humored attitude leads to a success-ful social life. Laugh with, not at, the people you socialize with and you can earn lifetime friends.

Use your creative thinking to inspire achievement. Humor can be used for creative problem solving and can assist you in becoming more flexible in your approach to your family, work and friends. Laughing with others helps you to appreciate their wit. Give others the chance to show off their creative thinking. Develop your humor ability by looking, listening and reading for amusing ideas, and examine situations to discover the unexpected. A woman who was given a windowless room apart from anyone else resolved her loneli-ness by putting a sign reading GENTLEMEN on her door! How can you use your humor power and creative thinking to solve your problems?

Humor Level

Humor, fun and laughter enrich your relationships. The more humor you include in your life, the more warmth and fun you can inject into each day. Recognizing your own separateness and differentness from others can be done in a humorous manner if you think of all human beings as electric appliances. Imagine that life flows through people just like an electric current, but here the similarity ends. The absurdity of expecting everyone to be alike can be better appreciated if you are aware that underneath our skins we are as different from each other as electric appliances. Each has its role to play in life and none are better than the others. Are you able to recognize yourself and significant others in the following list, and can you add other types to this list?

Refrigerator:	Crisply cool, with a large capacity for holding things in.
Freezer:	Frozen exterior, takes a long time to thaw.
Washing Machine:	Agitating and cleansing.
Dryer:	Tumbles others around with warmth.
Oven:	Someone who is really cooking.
Microwave oven:	Things are done much faster than expected.
Iron	Smooths things out.
Blender:	Whips things up.
Electric knife:	Most cutting.
Computer:	Analytical, uses head over heart.

Although presented humorously, non-recognition of the vital differences between people might mean that relationships become unglued because a "washing machine" is expecting a "refrigerator" to perform the same way. Examine the qualities of those close to you and be aware that each is performing in a way that is "right" for them.

Humor and laughter are powerful tools for healing and can be used in many ways to empower yourself. One method is to relax deeply and explore the inner you:

Imagine that you are sitting in a chair facing yourself. . .
Notice that you are laughing a great deal. . .
Your eyes are bright with laughter. . .
Now you are listening to a very, very funny joke. . .
All around you are sounds of other laughing too. . .
You can see someone you love laughing out loud. . .
And you are both laughing together at the funniest exper-
ience ever. . .

To live each day of your life more happily and to empower yourself, remember to bring past experiences of laughter to mind to improve the present.

Your Journal is another place to work on enjoying your sense of humor by writing your own humor, or collecting words and pictures of others. This section can be an excellent stress reliever in times of difficulty and a pleasure to reread. Include anything that puts a smile on your face to increase your humor level.

Each morning, frame your day by choosing a phrase for that day. For example, "This is a contented day," and color the day with pleasant emotion to make it come true. Put the phrase into your Journal and check at night to see whether you were able to stay within the frame you had drawn for your day.

Happiness and Power Level

To overcome feelings of unhappiness and powerlessness, close your eyes and experience deep relaxation.

Getting comfortable and breathing deeply, relax in a safe place. Now return to a time in your life when you felt wonderful. What were the tastes, sounds and smells? See an image of yourself very clearly; how you looked, how you felt, what you wore. Experience in your body all the emotions you felt; the laughter, the happiness and the joy. Locate in your body where you most strongly felt the happiness and permit that feeling to drain into your right hand; closing the hand tightly to experience the feeling of happiness and power. Let the image disappear and relax.

Now, double the sense of relaxation you are feeling by counting backwards to yourself, slowly, from five to one. Relax even deeper. Return now to a time in your life when you felt very unhappy and powerless; don't experience it too fully, just enough to be able to drain all those feelings in your left hand. Instead of clenching that hand, allow all the feelings to drain onto the floor. Let all the discomfort flow out of your body. Now let the whole scene fade and relax and experience a sense of calmness and peace.

Any time you experience any slight feeling of discomfort, first counter it with clenching your right hand and experiencing your power and happiness; then, slightly let in the opposite feeling and drain that from your left hand. Finally, clenching your right hand to re-experience feelings of happiness and power, let it spread from the top of your head to the tips of your toes. Notice how easily you respond to your beautiful self image.

In any difficult life experience, you can re-experience your power and happiness by closing your right hand and reliving the experience of happiness and power.

Love Level

This level is filled with dazzling light. It contains all the happiness and fulfillment anyone could desire. When you are fortunate to have someone to love who loves you, loving is easy. However, for love to exist, it does not require another person returning your love, it is wonderful when that occurs but not always necessary. Love can be a stream of love from you to a person, object or cause. Love given to a person such as a child, whether it is your own or someone else's, can bring sheer joy. Love of an object or symbol of beauty, such as a beautiful painting, mountain or ocean scene, can bring happiness. Love of a cause, whether political, educational or social, can bring satisfaction and happiness. With love the mind unfolds like a flower, effortlessly and of its own volition, and pulls you upward towards your highest potential.

Love of yourself will sustain you through life's difficulties. When you do not love yourself, you project this emotion onto others and see your shortcomings as belonging to someone else. The research on projection is immense. It seems clear that if projection works that way for hatred, then self-love would produce positive projection of feelings onto others. How powerful your interpersonal love relationships would be if from the cornerstone of loving, nurturing and caring for yourself, you would have a base for extending that love to other people.

A patient, with the loss of her husband, suffered deep grief and isolated herself from people. As a grandmother, she felt strongly she would never marry again and that love would be missing from now on in her life. After successfully dealing with her grief-work, she was able to extend her love to a small child living on her street. The child was too young to have a great deal to give the adult but the woman learned how good it felt to send her love out to the child each day in different ways. In time, she was able to enter into normal relations with her own family, but it was the seed of love for the neighborhood child which started this.

A man who lost a woman he loved to another man almost gave up on life and after some therapy, was able to reinvest his interest in his creative ability to paint. He found himself in union with the beauty of the things from nature that he painted. Surrounded by his work one day, he experienced the same stirrings within himself of peace, love and serenity that he used to experience with the woman he loved. It amazed him to recognize that there were many outlets for his love other than with that particular woman. With his artistic eye, as you might guess, in time he found himself able to love another woman and reinvest himself in her and his painting.

There have been people who have discovered the love of being involved in a political, educational or social cause. Getting involved with nuclear concerns was a political love of one woman. A man who invested his feelings in educational improvements in local schools found satisfaction in this area. A woman who obtained her degree in social work found her life fulfilled from working with runaway teenagers. Though previously she had not been involved with too many other people, in the work she did she learned to love these teenagers and received a great deal of satisfaction from the love they returned to her.

Recognizing that love comes in many forms will assist you to reorganize your love life in a way that is right for you. Your inner wisdom has the answer for you. Give yourself the opportunity to listen to yourself to learn how to expand your love level.

Enriching yourself at the love level answers profound inner human needs and reflects deep regard for the value of another person. Loving assists your personal evolution and maturity and is self-rejuvenating. History has not afforded many people the opportunities which are available today for choosing one's mate. In the past, the family, church or state, or financial considerations, would have selected the person you would marry and hopefully love. Today you can choose the person you wish to marry in the pursuit of your own happiness.

As you develop your personal identity and expand your awareness of who you are, you can experience taking more responsibility for your own existence and well-being as well as those you love. In improving your love relationships, you increase emotional closeness and intimacy. Successful love is an opportunity to give expression to your values, inner thoughts and goals. In valuing another, you in turn value yourself. In sharing your inner thoughts with another, they become alive and have greater meaning and you increase the probability of reaching your goals. Loving is a voyage of self-exploration and an adventure in exploring each other's depths.

Give yourself the opportunity to explore the various kinds of loving available in your life. Cultivate many perspectives and recognize the alternatives open to you in sharing your love, either with another individual, with beauty, or in a cause. Love comes as a by-product of sharing your happiness in living. People choose other people often on the basis of their love of life. Imagine that you can increase the brightness of your life to the extent that you are willing to increase the level of love you have to share.

Philosophy Level

An important part of your thinking process involves your philosophy of life. Whichever philosophy enhances your daily living is the right one for you. It may or may not involve religion. Some human beings prefer a non-traditional religious point of view, some a totally non-religious point of view, but it does not mean that they are not in touch with the spiritual dimension of life. For those people whose religious beliefs bring them comfort, happiness and spiritual satisfaction, then that is the right religion and philosophy for them.

In addition to traditional religions, it is possible to choose a philosophy which you have designed as your own. You may have chosen a philosophy which evokes the best in you. For example, you might choose to love a Supreme Being who defies explanation but who nevertheless enriches your life. What matters is that you have a philosophy of life that works to produce life satisfaction, integrated thinking and emotional stability. It is suggested that you write in your Journal what your philosophy or religious views are, writing about the ways that these views enhance your living. You might never have formally thought through what you believe and put it in writing. It is important for you to know where you stand so that these beliefs can support you in times of turmoil, as well as fill you with satisfaction at other times.

Your philosophy of life might include a point of view that the essence of you is perfect. There may have been behaviors which you have not done that you wished you had and things you did which you wish you had not. Nevertheless, there is part of you which is perfect and nothing you can ever do or not do can ever change that. When the person you are was given life, the ESSENCE of you was perfect and it will remain that way for all time. You are neither saint nor sinner, you are a human being struggling for excellence; sometimes failing and sometimes succeeding. And the ESSENCE of you remains perfect.

No matter what any other person may have said about you, the essence of you is inviolate. Someone calling you an airplane does not make you one even if you attempt to fly. So no matter what another's behavior might be towards you, in the main it only says things about that person; it does not say anything about you. The same is true of what a person might say about you, it does not change you. Return all unwanted comments back to the sender, secure in the knowledge that the ESSENCE of you is perfect.

The more you think through your philosophy of life, the more easily you are able to deal with life's fluctuations, secure in the knowledge that at all times, in all places, and under all circumstances, you are worthwhile and perfect as a result of being alive. You are struggling, doing the very best you can with the conditions you are living under at each precise moment. Based on the information you have, you are striving towards creating the best possible life for yourself; in spite of many detours, in spite of harming yourself or others, you remain perfect deep within the ESSENCE that is YOU.

Pleasure Level

Another level in building a new personality is the pleasure level. It has been found in working with animals that if they can press a bar and excite the pleasure centers in the brain, the animals will keep on pressing the bar until they are exhausted. Using imagery, it is possible to close your eyes and remember all the times in your life when you have experienced pleasure. Take one of the experiences, perhaps after loving, and re-experience that feeling now. It is possible, frequently throughout the day, to allow feelings of pleasure flow over your body as you remember a pleasurable experience. Recreating it again in your imagination allows you to relive in imagery the same pleasure, over and over again.

Without effort, negative thinking produces negative emotions and, consequently, negative behavior. With effort and positive, pleasurable thinking, you can produce positive behavior and more easily achieve happiness for yourself. This level would also include humor and laughter; the more easily you can recall humorous and funny events, the more this experience recreates pleasurable feelings in your body.

Right now, imagine for yourself a feeling you have experienced of pleasure. Imagine, with all your senses and with full emotion, what it would feel like to re-experience it in your body. Feel the emotion flowing through the whole of your body, permitting yourself full and complete enjoyment. Allow yourself to get in touch with those things which are rightfully yours: happiness, pleasure, joy, fun and laughter. Experience it vividly throughout your body and know that you can come to this level in the new building of your personality as often as you wish. It is a particularly good level to rise to away from the basement emotions and thinking which will lock you up in darkness. Instead, approach the light available to you on the pleasure level.

If you have tended to inhibit your ability to experience pleasure, now is the time to give yourself permission to enjoy your life. Experiment with your attitude toward pleasure and discover your potential for radiating enthusiasm. It is okay for you to abundantly enjoy each day of your life and produce states of pleasure for yourself frequently. Learn to let go and enjoy, without manipulation, those things which increase your emotional vitality. Pleasure can be found in each thing that you do when you choose to view it that way. Your aliveness as an individual is governed by your capacity for pleasure. Pleasant feelings let you know that you are moving in the direction of supporting your own strengths.

Meditation has been found to be effective for contacting your own potential for many things, including experiencing pleasure. You can learn to overcome your inhibitions and explore dreams and desires which would produce pleasure. Cultivate a way of seeing more alternatives and different choices available about most pleasures. Turn off the voice in your head that tells you to be afraid of too much pleasure. Take your freedom as a human being and trust yourself to go up to the heights of pleasure and then return responsibly to your other tasks. Give yourself mini-vacations of pleasure each day and evening, in whatever way you deem desirable. Living each moment presents you with the choice of experiencing pleasure NOW instead of putting it off to a time that might never come. It is not being suggested that you overthrow all social conventions and unnecessarily risk yourself or others in wild pleasure. What is being suggested is to allow yourself pleasure in an ongoing fashion daily. NOW is the time for you to experience living on the pleasure level.

Self-esteem Level

You can excel by working on this level to raise your self-esteem to where it belongs. Self-esteem can be raised by learning to:

1.   Be connected in significant relationships, by including others in your life. Also by including yourself in the lives of others.
2.   Be in control of your life by using your power to influence your life in a positive direction.
3.   Finding affection in your life; at home, work and play.

You are unique – sui generis – and the essence of you is of

incomparable value. No matter what has happened to you or your body which has been negative, the essence of you remains perfect. Ways to get further in touch with your own essence and raise your self-worth and self-esteem include:

1. Writing your life history only listing the positive events which you might have almost forgotten.
2. In this rewrite of your life, assign value and meaning to life events which you might not have recognized as being valuable when they happened. Often, negative-seeming events have good outcomes later in time.
3. Read to discover someone you admire and model your life after this person. Use this person as a psychogram, a model of the way you choose to be.

Integration of Higher Levels

Learning to flow between the levels described gives you an autonomy and personal power to use each day. Teaching yourself the difference between basement and higher levels of brain integration provides mastery and self control. You can remain stable, governed by the inner strengths you are discovering, as you build your *PERSONALITY PLUS.*

LEVEL 7: INTERMEDIATE LEVEL II
Creative Thinking

Creativing thinking is a major skill to be learned in the *PER-SONALITY PLUS* program. The cycle of creative thinking, rich imagery, positive emotions and new behaviors is intricately connected:

With the combination of skills you have learned so far, and will continue to learn, you will take a major step in changing your personality. Research confirms that the way you think affects your emotions, as does the visualization work which alters your behavior in the desired direction. For creating *PERSONALITY PLUS*, your thoughts are powerful tools. The level of thinking you are operating on can alter drastically when you change your thought patterns. Instead of permitting anxious or fearful thoughts to dominate your thinking, it is possible to change the outcome of events and your personal comfort by changing your thinking. Descriptions follow for avoiding negativity, managing stress, expanding brain power, re-labeling, reframing, personal creative thinking, and expanding trust.

Creative thinking involves taking a long, objective look at your-self, perhaps with the help of a mate or friend. Ask yourself how your thoughts have created the world as you see it. Thinking creates your relationships and your environment. It is our individual inter-pretation of each event which determines our response to the event. Taking responsibility for your personal, social and environmental surroundings puts them in a different perspective. If you are dis-satisfied with any of them, once you have taken responsibility for their existence, you then have the opportunity to create alternatives and make other choices. If your self-concept is causing difficulties, it can be changed to a more joyful world-view.

In your Journal, write out and analyze your current style of thinking. Search for ways to cultivate more creative thinking. Read-ing the ideas of others will enable you to synthesize their thoughts and come up with ideas of your own. Examine your belief systems to discover what your thinking is in important areas: What are your beliefs about personal matters? What social events are of importance to you? What is the environment like around you? The moment that you take responsibility for the way you have created your surroundings, you are put in touch with your own power to change things. The deeper you drill into your creative thinking ability, the wider your world view becomes.

There is a natural tendency towards creative thinking if you will clear the underbrush and allow it to emerge. As children, you felt freer to express your creativity and imaginative thinking but may falsely believe that with age, you have less ability to learn new skills.

In building a creative, internal environment, you can create fresh thinking. Through the use of relaxation and imagery methods described in this book, you can increase your selective awareness and focus your attention on your ability to think creatively.

Avoiding Negativity

Direct your creative thinking to pleasant and energizing thoughts. Thinking negative thoughts can be likened to carrying around a basket of snakes. They are similar to black, crawling snakes all interwoven in a tangled, slippery mass. Self-observation, when you are feeling depressed, will soon show you whether you are carrying around your particular basket of snakes. A basket of snakes was chosen because most people would not choose one snake, let alone a basket of them to carry around. Yet in a state of unawareness, you may carry around negative thoughts which can be much more harmful. Recognize that you have the ability at any given moment in time to park the basket or destroy it. Being aware that *you* have chosen to pick it up will, interestingly, remind you that you have the choice not to keep carrying it around. Next time you put down the basket, notice that you did it all by yourself, by choosing positive thought processes.

Thoughts and feelings are intricately connected; with the thoughts, no matter how fleeting, producing the negative emotion. When you next experience negative thoughts about any issue, take stock of the feelings of depression that accompanies them. Particularly notice when you need to master negativity by:

1. Turning fear into a challenge and a stepping stone.
2. Examining the stressors and how your thinking contributes to them.
3. Exploring expectations you have which might not be reasonable.
4. Restructuring your negative self-statements.
5. Reframing and relabeling the actions of others.

6.   Giving yourself gifts from your creativity.

Then, dropping negativity in your thinking, carefully setting aside your snake basket, notice how the draining feelings of depression, anxiety or fear disappear.

To handle anything you are afraid of, instead of sinking with it, use it as a stepping stone and as a challenge. Several examples from psychotherapeutic work are:

1.   A lady who was afraid of the disease her parents died of studied to be a doctor in order to treat that disease.
2.   A person who had a fear of flying overcame it by turning the fear around and trained to be a pilot.
3.   Someone whose cancer remitted used the experience to help others in the same situation.
4.   A woman fearing she would lose a relationship learned to recognize her dependence on her husband. From the fear of her own helplessness to support herself, she chose to develop her own career. The independence she developed improved the relationship between this couple.

Your greatest fear has within it the kernel of great potential for you if you will challenge the fear head on. Fear is just a deep breath away from excitement. When afraid, take a deep breath and feel the excitement of meeting the challenges of life. Thinking processes (self-talk) can strongly affect the transactions between physical, physiological, spiritual, social and psychological stressors. Learn to become aware of what you think and how it creates stress in your life. You owe it to yourself to keep any stress level only to the point where it motivates you to creative action, not debilitates you.

Many people have a great deal of trouble switching over from negative thinking to positive thinking and a midway point in this is discovering the NEUTRAL switch. Viewing the situaition in a neutral manner is the first step towards more positive thinking. As you become aware of negative thinking, put up a big STOP sign in your head to remind yourself how stressful negative thinking is for you emotionally. Then, until you learn to shift to a more positive view of what is happening, give yourself permission to remain in NEUTRAL on the issue until you can gather more data.

Human beings have an endless stream of thoughts and this self-talk often causes distress. Restructuring your thinking tapes is an effective way to change attitudes and behaviors. Begin by monitoring your inner dialogues to prevent self-critical and discouraging monologues. Stop negative self-statements and setting unreasonable standards for yourself and others. Avoid being dominated by anxiety and, instead, anticipate success. When you detect distress caused by depression and anxiety, instantly replay your self-statement and really hear what you are saying to yourself that is causing the distress. Instead of rigidly restricting yourself with such words internally as "Always" or "Never," learn that occasional relapses or failures are invaluable for developing coping skills.

Examine your expectations of yourself and others. Expectations require a very delicate balance. If your expectations of yourself are too high, you experience perfectionism. This expectation will create unhappiness and creates unnecessary stress. Keeping your expectations of yourself too low, on the other hand, results in unfulfilled potential; hence the need for balance in your self-expectations.

Expectations of others that are too high can create a lot of painful experiences and often lowering your expectations here also results in a more realistic approach. Make a list of the expectations you have of significant people in your life and see how many of them you can meet for yourself. Where you are expecting fulfillment of your needs from someone else, you keep yourself dependent. View supplying your own needs where possible as a way of developing your independence. If someone who looked after you in your childhood omitted some very important things you expected from them, ask yourself how you can supply them right now.

Managing Stress

Stress management is an important part of handling negative emotions. Merely by negative thinking, you pour out stress hormones excessively into your body: epinephrine, norepinephrine and cortisone.

Physiological damage is evident in such common complaints as ulcers, backache and headache. Negative thinking damages one's immunity to disease and contributes to such major illnesses as heart attacks, hypertension and brain strokes. We are discussing here life-threatening illnesses and you have much more to gain from changing your thinking processes than might appear on the surface. Anger, among other emotions, produces stress. Angry clients have inquired, "Why should I forgive those people, they were in the wrong," and an answer has been, "*You* will benefit yourself by forgiving them and that is reason enough to change your way of thinking." So, for yourself and family, become aware of negative thinking and how detrimental the stress hormones are to your health.

When you experience anger, rage, fear, anxiety or jealousy, for example, the sooner you can adjust your thinking to at least a neutral level, the sooner your body can adjust to the stressor. You may choose not to adapt but that puts the body in a state of resistance, using energy merely to combat what is happening rather than resolving it.

Think of a man who has the right-of-way in his car and another person runs the red light. The first man can insist, and he will be dead right if he crashes. It is better to adjust to the situation and let the person running the red light go on through. Life is like that, sometimes it makes more sense to adapt to the situation than to lose everything by insisting on being right. How you behave originates in your thinking processes and learning to control that area of life teaches you the self-control that raises your self-esteem. You benefit from the positive spiral in countless ways by controlling your thinking processes.

Brain Power

The human brain has evolved over billions of years and contains countless trillions of pieces of information. Despite evolution, the brain is limited in daily living by the amount of stored information which is available to it. There is a difference between stored and programmed information, in that with programmed information, you get to choose what your brain stores. Brain power is, with most people, an under-utilized asset. Expanding your thinking ability can drastically change your personality and your destiny. *PERSONALITY PLUS* is an opportunity for you to re-program your brain.

To learn to be in touch with your own subconscious brain, find a quiet place and focus on something above eye level. Allow the focus to be a soft one and in time you will find your eyes tearing or fluttering and they will tend to close. When this happens, try to see, inside the lids of your eyes, what you were gazing at with a soft focus. A soft focus is what sometimes happens when you are watching television and you experience the blending of two images. This concentrated attention allows you to focus inwardly when you close your eyes. To increase your feelings of relaxation, begin to count backwards from ten to one, imagining that you are descending on an escalator to a very safe place. In this relaxed state, when you have finished counting, you have access to your deep, inner mind.

The 90% of your brain power, which is not available to you in a conscious state, is readily available to you in a state of deep relaxation and inner reverie. You can extend your cognitive ability by learning to use your subconscious knowledge. On this level of concentration, you know much more than you are aware of consciously. You can reach within yourself and utilize your hidden brain assets at any time you choose.

Creative thinking involves awareness of your conscious and your subconscious mind. Consciously, the mind can become overloaded in its attempt to remember too many things at one time, yet it has incredible ability to recall specific events just by choosing to do so. The subconscious contains data on all your life experiences, and thoughts are used to retrieve whatever is stored there. Each time you choose a related series of thoughts, you have started a self-reinforcing process. Small thoughts, which by themselves are not bothersome, can with their own energy continue to build up unnecessary tension. In the same way, this process can be repeated with thoughts that are pleasant. Your task is to build a rhythm within your thinking processes which produces feelings of satisfaction and serenity. Focusing your attention on what you are thinking about produces an objectivity about the process and enables you to think adaptively.

The subconscious has the ability to simultaneously integrate and synchronize many more components than the conscious mind can handle at once. Learning that you can master what goes into your subconscious mind by monitoring your thinking gives you control of your subconscious processes. All of your emotions are affected by conscious and subconscious processes. Harmful thinking produces an ever-tightening spiral that puts you off balance; while simply altering your thinking can change your emotional responses. Breaking the cycle of chaotic thinking pays dividends of good, emotional health.

With the use of rich imagery, you can allow your mind to be receptive to pleasant thoughts. In the past, you may have been rewarded for linear, rational thinking and invalidated for using your imagination. Now is the time to allow your creative imagination to provide you with new thoughts. Setting aside time to allow your imaginative thoughts to bubble up from your subconscious allows you to use your full potential for creative thinking.

Relabeling and Reframing

What we call a thing, labeling, often determines future actions. On this level, you will be working on relabeling events in your life.

If we label a teenager's actions as rebellious and out-of-control, we are in a blaming, prosecuting mode of thinking. However, if we re-label the same teenager's actions as trying out his wings and struggling for his independence, we are more likely to have a better relationship with him and a better understanding of him. How we label the actions of those we love determines how we behave towards them. The next time you have a disagreement with someone, try relabeling what happened so that it has a better outcome.

Reframing a loved one's actions means putting their actions in a different context. If a husband insists that his mother visits for a month, instead of framing it as inconvenient, inconsiderate and mean of the husband, it could be reframed as showing love and care for his mother. Insofar as a husband can show these abilities to his mother, then he is more able to show the same affection for his wife and family. It is not always possible to treat everyone in a way that suits each individual, but if the individual who is unhappy with an event can learn to reframe that event in a more positive light he will benefit.

Your belief system in relation to what happens to you is what is important. In the case of the mother-in-law's visit above, it is not her visit which is the problem, but the wife's belief about it. If the wife can widen her perspective to include her husband's point-of-view, she can relabel and reframe the visit. Having self-control and refraining from denigrating this husband, the wife would enjoy increased self-esteem.

Personal Creative Thinking

Listening to your own thinking processes teaches you untold things about yourself. The amount of effort you are prepared to use to teach yourself the skills of productive thinking is directly in proportion to the benefits you will receive. Try an experiment: decide early in the morning that you will control your thinking for one whole day to experience having positive emotions. No matter what event occurs, keep yourself on track with your new method of

thinking. The harder you have to work at doing this, the more benefits you will receive for your effort. At the end of the day, ask yourself how the day would have turned out if you had not made the
effort. Then list, in your Journal, the pros and cons of this method.
Experience shows that the majority of people are impressed with
their own ability to develop personal creative thinking.

Creative thinking puts you in touch with your capacity for
greater happiness and greater aliveness. You can cultivate your enthusiasm for living by aspiring to think in ways which will produce
success as you define it. Thinking is the inner voice which tells you
constantly how things are with you. Is your inner voice telling you
that you deserve the best in life? Does it say that you can trust
your own judgment? Does it block self-nullifying statements and
allow you to develop positive, intuitive self-regard? Listen to yourself
by cultivating thinking which promotes feelings of happiness and
learn to operate with maximum power to achieve your goals.

Being in control of your thinking processes means that you pay
close attention to the choices which are available to you. It means
not shutting out possibilities by refusing to think through all areas
of important situations. People choose, for example, to remain depressed when, with a little effort, they could choose to get out of
the depressed situation. Except in major depressions which require
medication, there is a great deal which you can do for yourself in
depressing circumstances. Changing your thinking processes is an
important part of that work of enriching yourself.

Thinking creates autonomy and you can develop a deep trust
in your own thoughts. Your thinking can produce not only an
I-Thou feeling for you but also an I-Thou-Them outlook. By this
is meant that in an I-Thou mode, you recognize the uniqueness
and equality between yourself and others and when you change
that to an I-Thou-Them outlook, you are including in the interaction all the people who are connected with the other person in
the relationship. As an employer, for example, you can deal with a
subordinate as an equal while considering the effect of the workday

on the family of this person. Another example would be of dealing with a friend and not counseling him to act in a way that would be harmful to his family.

People are related to other people by invisible bonds and recognizing this in interpersonal relationships upgrades your thinking from what is right for "you and me" to what is right for everybody who will be affected by what is happening. Giving consideration to this as you think through work and home situations puts you at a higher level of thinking. This is a form of caring which produces feelings of well-being in relationships.

Trust

Basic to good interpersonal relationships is the establishment of mutual trust. Trust begins when you take the risk of disclosing your thoughts and feelings to someone else. If that person shows disrespect and ridicule or rejects your self-disclosure, this will destroy some of the trust in the relationship. If your trust and openness is received with support, acceptance and cooperativeness, the trust between you builds. Therefore, building trust in a relationship is being willing to respond in a supportive manner to the other person's risk-taking. This can be done by your expression of warmth and accurate understanding of what was shared with you. To increase the trust level between you can be done when you reciprocate with your own self-disclosures.

It is not always appropriate to trust and make yourself vulnerable when it would be destructive to your self-interest. Trust is only appropriate when you can be fairly confident that you will not be harmed or exploited and that it will be beneficial to trust the individual. Do not withdraw where trust is appropriate for by withdrawing, you set up a self-fulfilling prophecy. Take small risks to learn. where you stand in developing a trustworthy relationship.

Acceptance of yourself and others begins at the thought level. If you are giving yourself messages to behave in a guarded and suspicious way, others will reject you. If you monitor your thinking towards others and view them as friendly and trustworthy, you are initiating a warm climate for improved interpersonal relationships. Cooperative thinking draws other people to you as you express your trust in them. How you think is often apparent in your expression. Do you have a facial expression which shows trust in others? Is your expression guarded and unfriendly, or is it congenial and trustworthy? Cultivating thoughts with trust appropriately evokes trust in yourself and others and increases interpersonal warmth.

Learning mastery of your own thinking process will quickly show you many things which up until now have been peripheral to you, and will give you an opportunity to begin self-promotional thinking. You can examine your own philosophies and values to produce beneficial results. It is an opportunity for you to practice re-socialization of yourself for your own benefit. These gains can be achieved with slight behavior changes and are capable of producing fundamental personality changes. You can experiment in your work or at home by responding to two fairly similar situations in a different way and experience the difference in your emotions when you think in positive tones about the situation. Changing your thinking process has both short- and long-range effects on you and the people with whom you come in contact.

This program is strongly oriented towards recognition of your own human worth and self-acceptance. Carl Rogers gave psychology the concept of "unconditional positive regard" and you are invited to adopt this philosophy towards yourself. In learning to accept yourself unconditionally, you are asserting the fact that you are worthwhile because you are born; without conditions, without the approval of others, and without any other reason except that the essence of you is worthwhile. In excelling at self-acceptance, you are more able to accept others. It rarely works the other way around. Learning to discriminate between thought processes which hinder you, and those which promote your welfare allows you to remain calm and serene in spite of life's disappointments. Self-acceptance acknowledges your true humanity while you strive for excellence in your life to produce rewarding life experiences, not to prove you are worthwhile. You are worthwhile; allow your thinking to confirm it.

A way to express your personal freedom is to give yourself a "thinking pause" between anything that activates you to perform and the actual performance. Avoid trance-like responses to stimuli by becoming aware that even pausing for an instant gives you the opportunity to think of the outcome. Being a robot and responding from force of habit, without thinking of consequences and other options, decreases your awareness of what is influencing you.

Another way to learn the value of mastering your thinking processes is to use the odd-even method. On the odd days of a month, let your thoughts randomly follow their own pattern; and on the even days of the month, monitor your thoughts using the techniques for pleasant thinking that you have learned in this book. On the even days, it is anticipated that your days will have more emotional balance and you might be tempted to cultivate your thinking every day in order to reap the rewards. Negative thinking is like starting a spinning top, only a slight motion is required to get the top to begin; after a while, it spins of its own volition. This works the same way for positive, creative thinking. Use the image of the spinning top to start work on your even days.

Using the skills of awareness of what you are thinking gives you the key to unlock your own creativity. This creative exploration can stimulate you to find your own direction by thinking of new solutions to present and future problems. The greater the flexibility you permit yourself, the more options are available to you and any organism with the greatest selection to choose from has the survival edge. You can overcome reactivity by becoming an authority on yourself and a good place to begin is with your creative thinking.

LEVEL 8:   UPPER LEVEL I

Fresh Interpersonal Behaviors

Many excellent methods for fresh interpersonal behaviors originated in behavioral therapy and suggestions include their researched methods as well as methods from other disciplines. You are encouraged to develop each of the following changes in your behavior:

Assertiveness training	—	to avoid passive or aggressive acts
Communications	—	both verbal and nonverbal
Empowerment	—	experiencing your own uniqueness
High Achievement	—	reaching for your dreams

You will learn, from asserting yourself, how to negotiate so that each person involved wins. *Win-win* negotiation ensures good interpersonal relationships. Communication involves learning how to find pleasure in pleasing with words those people you interact with, and empowers you to give pleasure and nurturance to yourself. The highest achievement you desire can be yours. Aim for the highest mountain in the realm of what you wish to achieve and choose

99

behaviors that will bring you success. Maintain your flexibility by moving among the following levels as necessary and working on the segments which seem right for your *PERSONALITY PLUS*.

Assertiveness Training

Assertiveness is on a continuum, with Submissiveness on one end and Aggressiveness at the other:

Submissiveness　　——　　Assertiveness　　——　　Aggression

To learn which type of behavior you are using, ask yourself the following question, "How are my rights being handled?" If someone else is taking away your rights, you are behaving submissively. If you are taking away someone else's rights, then you are behaving aggressively. It is only when your behavior takes into account your rights *and* the rights of other people that you are behaving in an assertive manner.

To improve your assertiveness, you can practice when you are alone,using assertive responses where you might have been passive previously. Notice when you are aggressive in your responses and practice changing in mid-argument to an assertive stance — taking care of your rights and those of the person you are dealing with.

Assertiveness begins with an inner conviction that all communications are best based on *win-win* negotiations. Where your focus is *I-win/they lose*, you will make no long term gains with this aggressive stance. Where your focus is *I-lose/they win*, this causes you to be placed in a submissive, dependent role which will get in the way of your healthy, independent self-growth. There is an interdependency between those you negotiate with and it is healthiest when you examine the negotiation from the point of view of all participants. Expressing your point of view that this be a *win-win* negotiation, tells people up front that you would like to negotiate in the best interest of all parties.

Assertiveness is a skill which is learned from parents and peers and, in some families, boys were encouraged to be more assertive than girls. Wherever a person learned to be non-assertive, it is possible to develop assertive new behaviors. Rehearsal and change begin with learning which situations in life require an assertive response and practicing different responses. Begin by choosing a person whom you would like to be like and use this person as a model for practicing your new responses in imagination.

Practice, for example:

1.   Asking for a cash refund.
2.   Asking noisy people to be quiet.
3.   Telling a friend it is not a convenient time to talk.
4.   Asking for a raise.

Choose an item you would like to work with and begin by seeing the model you have chosen dealing with the situation assertively. Notice that this model chooses a simple, straightforward comment which asks directly what for what is wanted:

1.   I would like a cash refund for this item.
2.   Would you please be quiet.
3.   I am not able to talk right at the moment.
4.   I would like to discuss a salary increase with you.

See the scene in your mind's eye and see the model successfully completing the full transaction. From covert modeling of the situation, practice being assertive in non-risk situations and build up to riskier situations as your assertiveness blossoms.

Communication

The communication level of awareness is important in relationships. What you say and how you say it is as important as listening or being silent. Each communicates a message to others by words, non-verbal acting and by behaviors. What type of communicator are you?

Do you dance the tango in your relationship, both of you dancing but staying the same distance from each other? Does one of you follow and the other flee, and neither of you connect? Do you communicate as though back to back, neither hearing nor understanding each other? Do you communicate in another language, unaware that the other person doesn't understand what you are saying? Do you say or hear the same thing so often you have both stopped listening?

Describe in your Journal the type of relationship style you use to communicate to those close to you. Begin by describing it from any of the following and add your own description: Is the relationship Father/Daughter, Mother/Son, Rescuer/Victim, Leader/Follower, Controller/Controllee, Distancer/Pursuer, Rich Daddy/Baby; or how does it seem to you? All relationships involve a power struggle but they are not sporting events. Stop wrestling for control — there is no way to win this kind of match. If you find yourself in a power struggle, take control by letting go of your end of the rope. Relationships are pooling of resources. Learn to bend when communicating. Creating good communication takes patience and energy.

Learn to provide activities for yourself alone. Move aside from your partner and allow a separate space too. Notice your communication games and stop them. Good communication can be nurtured only in genuineness. Change your focus from what you get from the relationship to what you give. Provide your own self-esteem, growth, happiness and fulfillment. Don't expect others to be able to supply you with these things; it is your responsibility. Happy, long-lasting relationships don't magically occur, they require loving, tender, responsible communication and kind behaviors.

Many people report difficulty in communicating with significant others and strangers. Temporary or long-lasting relationships can be improved by noticing the tape running in the back of your head. This self-talk can provide you with all the data you need on how you are feeling and what you are experiencing. You can convert this self-talk in the following way:

1.   If you are warm, cold or hungry, instead of commenting on that, say, "How do *you* find the temperature in this room?

2.   Make sure you do not ask a *closed* question, a question which can be answered Yes or No, such as "Do you find this room warm?" Closed questions sometimes bring answers which terminate the conversation.

3.   Use small, social sentences to keep the conversation alive: "Tell me more," "Explain that further please," or "Describe what happened. . ."

Additional skill in communicating is learning the ability to listen empathically and feed back what the speaker just said. An individual really feels heard when you respond with a summation of what he just said. Often, if you will describe the feelings that the person just described using only one sentence, that is all that is necessary; such as, "That must have made you very angry (sad, disappointed, pleased) when it happened." Another way might be to say, "You must be feeling _____ over that." Actively listening to others and responding with empathic feedback improves interpersonal communication.

Communication skills can be increased by visualizing all the boundaries between relationships as concentric circles inside each other:

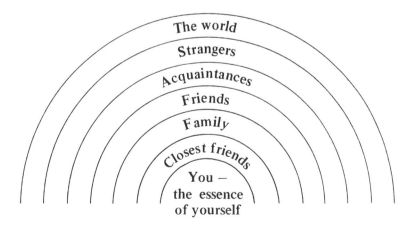

The world
Strangers
Acquaintances
Friends
Family
Closest friends
You –
the essence
of yourself

The outer circle is the world, the next inner one are strangers to you and the next inner one might be acquaintances. The circle inside that might be friends, then family and then closest friends. The very center of the circle is the essence of you and is rarely, if ever, shared with those in the outer circles, and may not be shared with many who are close to you. Keeping various people within the boundary for the particular relationship that is appropriate for both of you avoids intimacy problems.

Boundaries in relationships are very real. Observe the different boundaries between members of your families and friends to determine which ones are appropriate and which ones are not. Keeping the boundaries appropriate between yourself and others avoids being enmeshed inappropriately or too rigidly distant. Your aim is for clear boundaries, as described by Minuchin, which means that boundaries are permeable and that they change with circumstances. For example: enmeshment is appropriate between a new baby and mother and distance is appropriate between parents and adult children. Recognizing invisible boundaries which exist between ourselves and others gives mastery in relationships.

Good interpersonal relationships are attained by achieving a middle of the road stance in regard to intimacy. Here are two styles which prevent intimacy:

Overpersonal:
Being overly-candid and divulging too much personal material too soon in the relationship. Holding on too tightly to people so that they naturally struggle to get away. Being too friendly for the other person's comfort. The boundaries between self and others is too flexible. Approach is too hot and too strong.

Underpersonal:
Being too withdrawn, non-self-revealing, very remote and removed. The coldness serves to keep others at a distance.

Keeping people out of the inner boundaries where deep relationships are formed, with boundaries which are too rigid.

A style which is effective in dealing with others is the:

Balanced Personal:
Uses a degree of warmth appropriate to the relationship. Keeps in mind the other person's responses to make sure the intimacy is appropriate for that time, place and person.

When relationships go wrong, often it is because something inappropriate has been triangled into them. Krantzler wrote about the different things which are triangled in at various times in the relationship. Depending on which developmental stage you are in, there are a host of things which are triangled in which prevent intimacy between you and your partner. A new mother, for example, might triangle in her new baby. A distancing husband might triangle in work or lodge memberships. A retired couple might triangle in poor health and distance from each other over it. Examining what is between you and important people in your life and removing the triangled item will improve the relationships between you. At each stage in life there are challenges to be met and maintaining boundaries and a good balance of intimacy in your relationships are worth the effort.

Empowerment
Nurturing and empowering yourself is an important part of this program. Please look after your own needs with the same loving care that you look after the needs of others. You count. Pay attention to your own needs for rest, recreation, relaxation, diet, exercise and love. Acknowledge any human frailty and be kind to yourself.

You can empower yourself further by experiencing your own

uniqueness. There are visible signs of your uniqueness in your face and fingerprints but there is a less visible sign in your unique brain. The vast potentialities and complexity of the brain are only recently being recognized. Empower yourself by becoming aware of the great qualities of your left and right brain which will assist you to reach your highest achievement. Setting goals directs your brain to work on achieving your dreams. By the year 2,000, life expectancy will be approaching 100 years of age — you are in the prime of your life for setting future goals.

The effects of your efforts will reach further than you know. To empower yourself, be tolerant of any human errors you have made. For the hundreds of times your judgment has been right, applaud yourself. It is essential for you to have a positive view of yourself in order to enjoy your life to the fullest. Empowerment occurs when you network with your peers, when you mentor someone else in your field, if you are established, and when you share your knowledge with others.

High Achievement Level

On this level, you have access to your goal of high achievement — whatever you dream of, you can do. When you are on this level, don't list what you cannot do, instead argue for what you can achieve. Strongly visualize yourself at your maximum potential; experience it in your body, with rich tastes, sounds and smells, the YOU that you plan to be. Minor decisions can be made by weighing the pros and cons in writing, but in this area of high achievement, major decisions are best made by consulting your inner self.

So now, close your eyes, and open your inner eye of faith to see yourself at your highest level of achievement. Is the view breathtaking from there? If not, travel higher and imagine yourself at your *highest* level of achievement. Using the rich imagery described in this book, strongly experience your life goals. Then, after the imagery, write them out. Describe your life goals and the beginning, intermediate and final steps you will take to get there. Date your goals so that later you will be able to compare your growth as you expand your horizons. Answer the following questions:

1. What are my goals for the next one, five and ten years?
2. What steps will get me there?
3. When will I begin?
4. Does this feel right in the inner recesses of my mind?
5. Is this my highest dream?

Your Lifespan

Your thinking may determine your longevity and you are invited to explore the following factors in survival:

Physical activity

Making sure that you are physically active enough to keep your brain well oxygenated enables you to think in a healthy manner.

Sharing your experiences

Bottling up your distress quietly and passively accepting events without assertively thinking of ways to overcome them decreases your lifespan. Actively thinking of ways to share your distress with those who can help you extends your life.

Morale

Using your creative thinking ability to improve your morale means you will overcome depression, which can be a killer. Paying attention to your morale means actively thinking and behaving in ways to overcome depression. Keep your morale at the highest level and resist depression.

Interpersonal Relationships

Avoid isolation and loneliness, one of the largest inter-personal problems of adjustment in this country. Concentrate on nurturing the relationships you have and building new ones. Love relationships of all kind nourish your life and enhance your lifespan.

Commitments and Goals

Having commitments which involve other people's welfare as well as your own will enable you to have goals which are life-enhancing. Set aside time to creatively design, in your Journal, a well-thought-out program of suitable goals and commitments.

Utilize your brilliant, creative brain to achieve self-actualization by actively paying attention to your thinking processes on both a conscious and subconscious level. Your interpersonal relationships and life happiness depend on how you cultivate your creative thinking.

LEVEL 9:   UPPER LEVEL II

Refined Interpersonal Behaviors

You can discover how to refine your interpersonal behaviors by practicing the following new skills:

Interpersonal Behaviors — how your behaviors affect others
Here and Now Focusing — living in present time
Behavior Barometer — working in your own best interest
Comfort — the indoor/outdoor setting of your choice
Popularity —what it takes to be popular
Charisma — the indefinable attraction to others
Recognition — the effect it has on others
Sharing — giving of yourself to others
Fresh Behaviors — the accumulation of what you have learned

Taking note of your interpersonal behaviors improves your self-mastery and self-esteem. Here and now focusing means deleting the past and future in order to enjoy the present. Watching the barometer on your behaviors by checking stress level will increase your comfort in a setting that is conducive to your creativity. You can improve your popularity by recognizing and sharing yourself in a new and different way so that these fresh behaviors increase your interpersonal relationships and enhance your charisma.

Interpersonal Behaviors

A realistic evaluation of your behavior is necessary for you to be able to perceive which behavior it would be most advantageous for you to change. If you see yourself and the way you behave through rose-colored glasses, you may believe that no changes are necessary. If the way you are behaving is working for you, you are fine. However, if your interactions with other people cause you grief, taking action to change your behaviors will be in your own best interest. To begin building an accurate sense of your selfhood, evaluate where you are right now in interpersonal relationships and, in your Journal, describe the changes in behavior that are appropriate for you.

Your goal in undertaking behavior change is the development of a well-integrated, positive self-image. There are many positive features in your lifestyle and personality but, for most people, evaluating their behaviors would assist them to participate more fully in the world. Armed with information about yourself puts you in control of your behavior instead of leaving you at the mercy of the winds of chance. Instead of behaviors working out accidentally sometimes, you can ensure that your behaviors are more effective most of the time.

Self-control behaviorally increases your self-esteem: that sense of personal efficiency and a sense of personal worth. People experience different levels of self-esteem and everyone has the capacity to grow further in self-trust and self-reliance. Your level of self-esteem affects your behavior in relationships. Improving your self-concept will determine your destiny, as will improving your behaviors. Being aware of the messages you send, by the way you behave, gives you the advantage of being in control of the situation. It will help you to take off the blinders to the roles you are playing in creating situations that you would have preferred to avoid.

To take responsiblity for your relationships, by observing your behaviors, is the first step to change. Surprisingly, many people believe that if they did not mean their communication or behavior, they are excused from it. To promote change, it is suggested that you examine your behavior in line with the *effect* it has on the other person. If your communication and behavior is damaging to the relationship, you owe it to yourself to change. Behavior is not discrete and separate. Each piece of behavior is similar to a small stone thrown into a pond. . .the rippling effects extend across the pond. Worse yet, if the behavior is bad, there are hidden effects underneath the water which will seriously affect your interpersonal relationships. Notice, too, that you cannot remove the stone or the ripples.

As human beings, we often find it painful or impossible to self-reflect; yet self-reflection is necessary if improvements are to be made in our behaviors. What the outcomes are of what we say and do to others is important data for us to have. Losing acquaintances and friends does immeasurable damage. If you look at what you have benefited from other people, you will realize how much you would have lost without them. There is no way to calculate what you have lost along with contacts, because there is no way to guess what might have transpired. Chances are, though, that there would have been much good in it for you. Take the time to monitor your behaviors to make sure that they build the type of personal contacts which enhance your life as you are developing your new personality.

A way to successfully deal with other people is to observe the patterns of their behavior on their own and their behavior in relationship to you. Only when you can understand what triggers responses in other people can you learn how to trigger the best behavior from them. Only as you learn what triggers your own behavior can you develop new behavior responses.

Observing others involves determining what types of roles they play in interactions. There are times when it is appropriate to play the role of clarifier, initiator, arranger, encourager, compromiser or harmonizer, while it may be inappropriate to be a blocker, conformist, emoter, avoider or challenger. This appropriate role depends on the situation, sometimes it is better to play follower than leader. Other times it is appropriate to use stereotypic sex-role behavior and sometimes not. Taking the best of both sex-roles would appear to be the most advantageous of behaviors.

Take inventory to see whether you are a fighter or abdicator; do you play God; or do you apologize and defend yourself? Do you play avoider or are you a negotiator? Your attitude and behavior, which is part of what other people see as "you," can be seen most clearly in stress or conflict situations. For your own benefit, it is helpful if you can see yourself as you appear to others. Playing ostrich about your own behaviors means that other people can still see you even when you think they cannot.

Behavior towards others is most effective when it results in *win-win* negotiations. *Win-lose* negotiations occur when there is suppression or denial of difficulties and the negotiators withdraw. Using power and dominance to win will also result in a *win-lose* outcome. Teaching yourself the art of compromise and negotiation, in order to collaborate, means learning to recognize the other person's position and making sure that they do not lose in the transaction. This often means each person giving way on some points in order to meet midway and produce a *win-win* outcome.

Win-win skills include being empathic towards the person you are negotiating with and building empathy and rapport, and bringing your best judgment into the situation. Decisions are made from attentive listening with an attitude directed towards solving the issue. Paraphrasing what the other person is asking for leads to better understanding of the issues. Stating clearly, at the beginning, that you are operating from a *win-win* perspective will facilitate new behaviors and success in negotiating.

Your behavior is often perceived nonverbally. The nonverbal behaviors are disclosed by your facial expression and body postures, your general health and your method of shaking hands. In addition, the tone of your voice changes the message you are sending drastically. For example, "You are beautiful," is a complement, but with a question mark at the end and a raised voice, the message changes. Become aware of how you look; do you walk and sit straight? Do you talk with assurance? Do you appear attentive and accessible? The more you know about how you talk, move and act, the more easily you can change your behavior to improve your interpersonal relationships.

In your behavior, you can model from someone you admire very easily by practicing small parts of their behavior until they become natural. Role-play, in your imagination, behaving like someone you admire. See, hear and feel yourself with their skills and practice them to make them your own. How you dress, stand and sound says a great deal about you. Cultivate behaviors which send out positive messages about you.

Here and Now Focusing

Focusing on the *here and now* is hard to do because we present ourselves with pictures from the past of the way things were and pictures of the future of the way we want things to be. However, to learn to be present in the here and now, what helps is to go home and empty all the garbage in your closets. Throw away all the things you are storing for which you have no use. Do one room at a time or one piece of excess baggage at a time, but do it. Sometimes garbage from the past takes away all the color from life and makes it black and white. Get rid of the garbage and add back the color into your life. Now you are probably going to laugh and probably won't be willing to throw away garbage from the past, but it is a way to focus on the here and now and be present in your current relationships. Don't overload yourself with behaviors from the past but set yourself free by giving yourself an uncluttered, fresh start.

Behavior Barometer

You can use the level of your stress to indicate to you whether your behavior barometer indicates you are working in your own self-interest. If the barometer shows a high stress level, this is an indication it is time to change your behavior patterns. See if you can recognize your behavior from the following types:

Over-Achiever

Do you measure your life by material possessions, status and accomplishments? Are you stressed to compulsively drive yourself, with an overscheduled day that leaves you fatigued? Do you measure what you are worth by what you earn?

Your first task is to convince yourself that you are worthwhile or that others are as worthwhile, no matter what your accomplishments. It is time for you to evaluate the importance of people in your life and place people before profit. You and others are worthwhile because you exist as human beings. Developing intimacy with others and separating your work and love life are behaviors which are more beneficial for you and your health.

Rager

Are you chronically angry, hostile and sarcastic? Are you so afraid of your true feelings, both negative and positive, that you hide them? Do your angry feelings break out unpredictably towards someone you care about when the real cause is something else? Have you chosen an adversarial stand and view the world as hostile to you?

Your first task is to learn to deal with your anger, using the exercises in this book, and learn not to use aggression and hostility towards others. Become aware of your tendency to alienate people and change your behavior to win them over.

Worrier

Do you run a tape through your head endlessly worrying about everything, creating panic and anxiety for yourself? Do you view life as an endless catastrophe? Do your negative thoughts attract other negative thoughts and place you on a downward spiral of worrying thoughts?

This internal behavior creates stress-inducing emotions and prevent you from rationally solving your problems. You may superstitiously believe that worrying about your problems will prevent the worse from happening. Worrying handicaps you from making decisions or acting on them. Instead of being preoccupied with worrisome thoughts, change this behavior to making decisions and acting on them. Learn to discard your superstition that worrying will prevent catastrophes from happening. Use your PERSONALITY PLUS skills to take actions to avoid catastrophes and learn to turn off worrying thoughts.

Pleaser

Do you remain passive in the face of other people taking away your human rights? Or do you freely give up your rights? Are you intimidated by authority and suffer from feelings of helplessness? Do you continue to smile and agree to do things that are not in your own best interest? Do you listen to your inner voice criticizing yourself but never other people?

Your first task is to learn how to do things which are in your best interest. Forgo smiling and feeling like a victim or martyr as you agree to do things you do not wish to do. People will still love you, perhaps even love you more, as you learn to say NO to unsuitable demands. With the skills you are learning, develop a plan which puts your needs as the number one priority.

Procrastinator

Do you engage in self-defeating behaviors by indulging in habits that are harmful; such as drinking, smoking and overeating, to compensate for the guilty feelings of procrastinating? Do you also engage in putting off tasks that you know have to be done? Do these behaviors sabotage your good intentions?

Your task is to learn self-discipline and learning to say NO to your impulses to gratify yourself by procrastinating. On the one hand, you put off what must be done and you indulge, on the other hand, in behavior which is best not done. Putting more balance in your life by changing your behaviors gives you the opportunity to overcome these tendencies.

Leaner

Do you depend on others to supply you with your needs, which you could learn to supply for yourself? In remaining dependent, do you cut off your own potential and creativity? How high is the price you pay for depending on others? Imagine, for a moment, that you were the person who was being leaned on and get a feeling of what it would be like to spend your days carrying someone else around. Experience the feeling of someone hanging on your neck and weighing you down, and get a sense of how much this behavior drains the carrier.

Take the time to start learning to be self-dependent and experience the feelings of increased self-esteem this generates. Try out your wings as an independent operator in small ways and teach yourself to get what you need out of life for yourself.

There are times when it is appropriate to play any of the behavior types described, but not to the point where it is self-nullifying. It is appropriate to achieve, for example, but not at the expense of one's intimacy and love interests. Being angry can be appropriate against injustice or poverty. There are rarely times when it is helpful to be a worrier, leaner or procrastinator, and this behavior can be changed. It is appropriate at times to please people but not at the expense of your own humanity. Ask yourself if your behavior fits into a category which is detrimental to your well-being and if so, write in your Journal the ways in which you plan to change it. Learn to overcome destructive tendencies and use your inner strength to behave in a way that produces appropriate behavior for your own health.

Comfort Level

In the building of your new personality, design a floor exactly as you would like it to be. Design it with an outside environment or an inside motif. If you have an outside setting which pleases you immensely, decorate it that way. Or, if you prefer, arrange to decorate it with an interior design motif. Whatever the setting which would please you immensely, make the comfort level that way. You might choose a combination, for example, by having your favorite furniture with plants and a waterfall, including whatever exterior and interior design that is right for you.

Use your enriched imagery to see, hear, smell, taste and touch the place which will bring you a feeling of great comfort. Experience what it feels like to be in this lovely, safe and relaxing place. Design it so that you would recognize it instantly as being your very own, complete with every luxury that you could desire. Splurge on providing everything you have ever wanted for comfort.

In classes, students have designed this level in many different ways:

- A modern setting with paintings and lighting to match. Lightweight furniture and scattered rugs on polished floors.

- A mountain top with pine trees nearly touching the clouds. The smell of pines, surrounded by rocks covered in pine needles.
- A cottage setting with corner fireplace, with comfortable country furniture.
- A mixture of traditional and modern furniture, in a modern glass dome, with much of the outside appearing to be inside.

Other people have designed their comfort level to include:

- A lake near the glacial mountains, fishing for trout or bass, on a day when the water is like glass.
- An area full of entertainment, dancing, games; to be occupied with many friends.
- An ocean home, with waves pounding the shore, and the sounds of birds circling overhead.
- A Victorian room in a city from long ago, with all the elegance of the nineteenth century.
- A forest, with ferns, with redwoods reaching to the sky, and thick moss to lie on under the trees.

As you can see from the comfort levels chosen, there are endless ways you can furnish your comfort level in imagery. However you visualize it so that it provides you with a feeling of comfort is all you are concerned with. It does not have to please any other living person, just yourself. In your imagination, you can transport whatever type of surroundings you choose to your comfort level. When you need to be there, you can allow yourself to enjoy the comfort you have chosen for the enhancement of your personality.

Popularity Level

For improving your popularity, let me share a secret with you.

You will be popular if you *behave as if you are*. People respond to your view of your own self-worth and if your behavior proclaims that you feel popular, you will be. Learn to listen to and accept compliments on your accomplishments. Don't place yourself among the people who might criticize your actions. Place yourself on the top of the list of people who are in your corner.

> *Close your eyes and imagine that you are on a stage placed before a large crowd of people. Notice that the audience contains many members of your family, friends and acquaintances. See them clearly. Now notice that everyone in the audience is applauding, including me, and experience knowing that everyone rates you highly. You are a success and are on top of the world. Hear the cheers and know that to many people, you are a very important person. Notice that the entire audience is standing, clapping and cheering. You are fantastic and you have it made.*
>
> *Now imagine that there is a golden connection between you and everyone present. Experience the feeling, strongly, of knowing that you like each other. You can be the center of the universe if you will allow yourself to be. Imagine that you have all the popularity you will ever require for happiness. Soak it up like a hungry sponge soaks up water; feel it in your pores as popularity enters your body from every direction. Feel yourself smile, taste the great taste of success, smell the warmth from your audience, hear the applause as you experience, once and for all, your own popularity throughout your entire body, mind and spirit.*

Charisma

Charisma is that indefinable something that we find attractive in other people. Brain chemicals, norepinephrine and dopamine, appear to create the emotional reaction of pleasure to the total impact of YOU. To improve this chemistry, be responsive to relaxation methods which will relax you and relieve anxiety in new situations. Body relaxation can be achieved by breathing in and saying silently, "Happy, healthy mind," and breathing out saying, "Relaxed, healthy body." Using this en route to a social event prepares you optimally for it.

Your body language should suggest openness as you avoid folded arms, rigid posture or a cold facial expression. Incline your body to the person who is speaking and feel friendlier towards them. Use your mind to give emotional feedback to what a person is saying, by repeating the last few sentences using other words to let that person know you heard what they were saying. For example: "You are sounding really delighted over what happened." Make sure that you do not interject irrelevant personal data which prevents the person from completing their communication.

Making eye contact, with inwardly smiling eyes, will let the other person know you are interested, There are ways of touching which are acceptable, ways to let the other person experience warmth and understanding. Become aware of how you sound; sometimes lowering your voice is very pleasing, as is a pleasant accent. Notice how you breathe, what rhythm your voice has, and your volume. Use words that are pleasing to the ear. Hearing and smell both provide charismatic effects. We are very nostalgic over perfumes and can remember them longer than what we see or hear. Perfume can have an hedonic effect. Be approachable, act in a friendly manner and smile. You can be as attractive to others as you wish if you are willing to let them experience your aliveness.

Recognition Level

It surprises many people to learn that among human beings, the greatest need is recognition. You might be tempted to believe that safety, love and food would rate among the highest needs a person has. However, indifference can kill a person psychologically and is felt more deeply than being hated. To be ignored by one's peers, or by someone you love, is a deeply painful experience. It is possible that you might get so wrapped up in your own life that you forget to acknowledge the people around you. Learn, on the recognition level, to give each person acknowledgment as a human being. Recognize a person's family, his job, his interests, his achievements, or his inner self and you will open up the doors of friendship that might otherwise have been closed to you. Giving others the recognition they need will bring you all the recognition you need and give you security in relationships.

You can build the skill of giving recognition by:

1. recognizing the other person's needs and feelings.
2. increasing communication skills of understanding each other.
3. mastering your thought processes to include recognition skills.
4. developing a program from self-to-other centered communication.
5. keeping a list of positive subjects for social conversation.
6. forming a bond with others by accepting them for what they are.

Remember, in your dealings with others, man's strongest craving is for recognition of his worth from his fellow man.

Sharing Level

This is the level from where you can examine what you have to share. You can network with others to see how you can assist each other, coming from abundance. You have more than material things, you have friendship and love to share. Check your supplies; what do you have that you can freely give? If you are older, what has the wisdom of the years taught you? Are you willing to share from the wealth of your wisdom with those who are less learned than you? If you are younger, are you willing to open your ears and eyes and take the gifts offered to you by the older generations?

Often there are material gifts which you have but do not need. Go into your attic and see what you are keeping that you will never use that perhaps someone else can use. What things in your home are cluttering up your space and how can you utilize these things for the benefit of others? Look carefully and see what you have to share. Sharing of yourself is a powerful gift and opening up yourself to this can be very rewarding. Are there places you can go where people would welcome your visits? Are there things you can do that can be done by no-one else? Use the power of your inner, subconscious mind to show you creative ways that you, and you alone, can share the gift of yourself.

Fresh Behaviors

List, in your Journal, the new behaviors you have incorporated into your life as a result of exploring this level. Cultivating each one of these skills in a meaningful way enables you to develop the *PERSONALITY PLUS* you can use in the Penthouse Suite.

LEVEL 10: PENTHOUSE SUITE

Your Highest Level of Competency

Now that you have pressed the elevator button and arrived at the Penthouse Suite, how does it feel? All the skills which you have acquired should by now have paid dividends in your life. At this level, compliment yourself on your ability to work closer to your highest level of competency. The road to success is always under construction. Your work will continue as long as you nurture the *PERSONALITY PLUS* seeds which you have planted to allow the miracle of YOU to unfold. The goal of *PERSONALITY PLUS* has been introducing YOU to YOU and it is hoped that you are enjoying your newly-tapped brain power. Accept what you have learned as your gift to yourself. Since practicing new skills, you have journeyed a long way in self-discovery. Your success and happiness is not a destination, it is a process. You are always in the process of becoming more of who YOU are. May you receive what you want for yourself in abundance.

Relax, close your eyes and breathing naturally, prepare to listen to your tape of the following:

Now, and in the future, accept the parts of your personality as an integrated whole, a new PERSONALITY PLUS, as you continue to say YES to life each time you relax.

Imagine it is very early morning and the sun in beginning to rise in the milky white and blue sky. You are standing in a beautiful meadow surrounded by tall pine trees. The scent of pine fills the air. Pine cones are lying on the floor and pine needles soften the sounds of your feet as you walk. The grass sparkles from the morning dew. Birds chirp to each other and nearby, a golden beach leads to a large, serene lake. The lake is surrounded by snow-capped mountains. The stillness and clarity of the water creates a sense of peace as you breathe in the beauty of the scene. You breathe in again deeply and breathe contentment and peace. Gentle breezes blow across the lake and warm your face.

Your humanity seems at once minute and magnificent. Minute in your smallness in relation to the mountains and trees. Magnificent in the richness of life and living that you experience. You are filled with happiness, serenely calm and in touch with all the earth and your own humanity. The richness of existence is here for the taking. All you will ever need from life, the strength, nourishment and warmth, the love and a sense of belonging, are here in abundance. Reach out and take your share of this superb beauty. Make a space within your body for this feeling, knowing that anytime you need it, you can get in touch with your own magnificence and remember this feeling. You can reach within yourself and say Yes to Life.

At this time, if you have followed the suggestions in this book, you will have:

- a thick Journal of notes describing the personality you are achieving.
- an understanding of the effectiveness of rich imagery.
- various relaxation methods for relieving stress.
- knowledge that your thinking alone produces your emotions.
- a clearer picture of your creative, daimonic potential.
- a means to deal with negative emotions, such as anger.
- an appreciation for the power of your subconscious mind.
- ways to meditate and relax to reach the inner YOU.
- ability to move to different levels of thinking.
- ability to incorporate compassion and courage to desensitize grief and pain.
- a strengthening of your self-control by mastery of emotions.
- increased your creative thinking.
- improved your interpersonal behaviors.
- ability to transform your irrational thinking to rational thinking.
- flexibility in moving between personality levels as appropriate.
- a strong desire to operate from your Penthouse Suite.
- enhanced and created your own *PERSONALITY PLUS*.

These abilities and many more are within you, and to the extent that you are using your best efforts to integrate these skills into your lifestyle, you will have achieved *PERSONALITY PLUS*.

On the Penthouse floor, you are on top of your world. Your total experiences feel different on this level of operating. You are learning to increase use of right hemispheric skills to complement your left hemispheric abilities. You can see people, places and things with clearer vision, and understand more how these operate in relation to each other. Your inner self has contributed to a new self-image which gives you mastery and self-control.

On this level, events sound different for you have learned to listen to your inner self with fresh understanding. You appreciate the taste and smell of success as you incorporate important new skills into your repertoire. You have a new sense of self. Stay in touch with your own power to use your *PERSONALITY PLUS* to create for yourself unlimited possibilities.

A personal message to YOU from the Author.

Let me compliment you on the hard work you have done using the methods outlined in PERSONALITY PLUS. You have learned by doing and will continue to grow as you apply the new skills to greater areas of your life. I would like to know you personally and would appreciate learning how you have applied this book to your life. Let me hear of your successes; I will value your communications.

Lynne O'Neill Hook, Ph.D.
783 Steuben Drive
Sunnyvale, California 94087
408-245-2677

SUGGESTED READINGS

Bloomfield, H. H. and R. B. Corey, *Inner Joy* New York: Wyden Books, 1980.

Ellis, A. and R. A. Harper, *A New Guide To Rational Living.* North Hollywood, CA: Wilshire Book Company, 1971.

Krantzler, M. *Creative Marriage.* New York: McGraw-Hill, 1981.

Koestenbaum, P. *Managing Anxiety.* Englewood Cliffs, NJ: Prentice Hall, 1974.

May, R. *Love and Will.* New York: W. W. Norton and Company, Inc., 1969.

Minuchin, S. and H. C. Fishman, *Family Therapy Techniques.* Harvard Press, 1981.

Rogers, C. R. *A Way of Being.* Boston: Houghton Mifflin Co., 1980.

Samuels, M. and N. Samuels, *Seeing with the Mind's Eye.* New York: Random House, 1975.

Zdenek, M. *The Right Brain Experience.* New York: McGraw Hill, 1983.